GRAM MAE'S
COLLECTION OF
FAMILY
RECIPES
AND LOVE
FROM HER
SOUTHERN
KITCHEN

WYNDHAM HOUSE

D1664833

Published by
Wyndham House, Inc.

NOTE FROM THE AUTHOR

I love writing the Tessa Lamar Novels. The main character, Tessa's quirky and fun, and lives in a world I miss dearly. A time when kids played outdoors and families gathered for dinner every night. I hoped to capture some of *the good old days* in these recipes.

One of my favorite things about being an author is receiving notes from my fans. I'm always blown away when readers say my characters reminded them of their own families. Gram Mae, in particular, seems to have struck a chord.

My only explanation for her popularity is the fact I based her on my Great-Grandmother Mae. She was the type of woman who could drop a deer or a shot of whiskey in one shot. She grew strawberries in an old John boat that washed up during a hurricane. The real Mae raised five girls, and countless grandchildren and great-grandchildren.

My fondest memories of her involve her humor, her love, and her little rose-shaped soaps. She's been gone over thirty years, but I still tear-up when I smell rose oil or drive past Sandy Lane in Apopka, Florida.

Gram Mae's Southern Kitchen is filled with recipes, wisdom, and love from my family to yours. Most of the dishes in this book are from my personal stash of favorites. Some are attributed to friends and family members, some include memories of times when I served the food, and others contain helpful hints and advice. Oh, and of course, I peppered in plenty of book quotes to make it fun.

Enjoy!
Kathryn

Find out more about me and my books.
www.kathrynmhearst.com

ALSO BY KATHRYN M. HEARST

Tessa Lamar Novels

The Spirit Tree

Twelve Spirits of Christmas

The Spirit Child

Sinistra Dei Series

Feast of Reverence

Feast of the Epiphany

Feast of Mercy

Feast of Atonement (Summer 2018)

Feast of Ascension (Fall 2018)

Zodiac Shifters

Dragon Glass

Contemporary Romance

Going Dark

Bourbon Street Bad Boys Club Series

(Coming soon)

TABLE OF CONTENTS

BREAKFASTS

I slipped out of the house before he woke and hightailed it to Mae's for breakfast. Carbs and fat were a poor substitute for a roll in the hay, but I would take what I could get.

— *Twelve Spirits of Christmas*

ANGEL BISCUITS

I believe this recipe was originally published by Betty Crocker. It's all over the internet. I found it in an ancient family cookbook.

1 package regular or quick active dry yeast (2 1/4 teaspoons)
2 tablespoons warm water (105° to 115°)
2 1/2 cups all-purpose flour
3 tablespoons sugar
1 1/2 teaspoons baking powder
1/2 teaspoon baking soda
1/2 teaspoon salt
1/2 cup shortening
About 1 cup buttermilk
Butter or margarine at room temperature, if desired

Preheat oven to 400°. Dissolve yeast in warm water; set aside. Mix flour, sugar, baking powder, baking soda and salt in large bowl. Cut in shortening, using pastry blender or crisscrossing 2 knives, until mixture looks like fine crumbs. Stir in yeast mixture and just enough buttermilk so dough leaves side of bowl and forms a ball.

Place dough on generously floured surface; gently roll in flour to coat. Knead lightly 25 to 30 times, sprinkling with flour if dough is too sticky. Roll or pat 1/2 inch thick. Cut with floured 2 1/2 inch biscuit cutter. Place about 1 inch apart on ungreased cookie sheet.

Bake 12 to 14 minutes or until golden brown. Immediately remove from cookie sheet. Brush with butter. Serve hot.

BAKING POWDER BISCUITS

Don't have yeast? Make these instead. They're not as fluffy, but they'll do in a pinch.

2 cups all-purpose flour
1 teaspoon salt
4 tablespoons shortening
2/3 cup milk

Heat oven to 425°. Sift flour, baking powder, and salt. Cut shortening into flour mixture. Add milk and stir quickly with a fork until a soft dough forms. Don't over stir! Knead 6-8 times, forming a ball. Roll out the dough on a floured surface and cut into circles with a glass. Bake 12-15 minutes.

BLUEBERRY FRENCH TOAST BAKE

This is heaven in a baking dish!

1 16 ounce loaf French bread cut in cubes
1 cup blueberries (fresh or frozen)
12 large eggs
1/3 cup maple syrup
2 cups milk
Sauce
1 cup sugar
1 cup water
2 Tablespoons cornstarch
2 cups blueberries (fresh or frozen)
1 tablespoon butter

Preheat oven to 350° Arrange the bread cubes in a greased 9 x 13 pan. Sprinkle blueberries evenly over the bread cubes.

Whisk together eggs, milk, and maple syrup. Pour over bread cubes and cover pan with foil. Let chill in refrigerator overnight.

Bake covered with foil in a preheated 350 ° oven for 40 minutes. Remove the foil and bake for another 20 to 30 minutes or until golden. Top with blueberry sauce.

For Sauce Combine the sugar, water and cornstarch until smooth in a small saucepan. Bring to a boil over medium heat; cook and stir until thickened, 3 minutes. Stir in blueberries; bring to a boil. Reduce heat and simmer until berries burst, 8-10 minutes. Remove from heat; stir in butter. Serve with French toast.

CHOCOLATE STRAWBERRY CREPES

These are wonderful to make for your sweetheart on Valentine's Day for breakfast or dessert.

For the Crepes
2 cups milk
2 eggs
3 tablespoons oil or melted butter
1 teaspoon vanilla extract
1 1/2 cups all-purpose flour
1/3 cup unsweetened cocoa powder
2 tablespoons sugar
A pinch of salt
1 cup heavy cream
3 tablespoons powdered sugar
I pound strawberries, sliced

Blend the milk, eggs, oil/butter and vanilla extract until combined. Add the flour, cocoa powder, sugar and salt and blend until smooth. Refrigerate batter for 1-2 hours or overnight.

When you are ready to make the crepes, heat a large griddle or skillet on medium heat. Lightly brush melted butter on the pan. Pour 1/4 cup batter in the pan and swirl the pan so that the batter evenly covers the bottom. Cook the crepe until bubbles appearing on the surface. Flip the crepe when the edges turning a light golden brown. Cook the other side for a few seconds. Remove from pan and place on a plate. Repeat till all the batter is used up, stacking the crepes on the plate.

To make the filling, mix or whisk the heavy cream and powdered sugar in a cold bowl until soft peaks form. Spread a couple of tablespoons of whipped cream mixture on one half of a crepe. Dot with sliced berries. Roll or fold and dust lightly with powdered sugar. Repeat with all crepes. Serve at room temperature or cold.

Gram Mae's Secret: *Swap the whipped cream for Nutella, peanut butter, or syrup.*

EGG IN A NEST

Fried eggs in a toast nest. I remember thinking these were the fanciest eggs that had ever graced a plate when I was little.

1 egg
1 slice of bread
1 tablespoon butter
Salt and pepper

Crack the egg into a bowl and set aside. If you're like me and hate runny eggs, scramble the egg now. Use a cookie cutter, or rim of a glass, to cut a shape out of the piece of bread. Any shape will work, as long as it doesn't cut the edges of the bread.

Melt the butter in a frying pan over medium heat. Place the bread in the pan and fry it lightly on one side. Toss the cut out shape in the pan, too. Flip the bread over. Reduce the heat to low.

Pour the egg into the hole in the middle of the bread. Season the egg with salt and pepper. Cover the pan and cook for about 2 minutes or until the egg has set.

FRENCH TOAST BREAD PUDDING

I first had French Toast Casserole at a Bed & Breakfast in Savannah, where my daughter and I celebrated her 13th birthday. It took a few test runs, but I managed to capture the flavors.

1 cup brown sugar
1/2 cup butter
1 (8 ounce) loaf crusty French bread, cut into bite-size pieces, or as needed
2 cups milk
6 eggs
2 teaspoons vanilla extract
1 pinch ground cinnamon, or to taste
1 tablespoon brown sugar, or as needed

Grease a 9x12 inch baking dish. Stir brown sugar and butter together in a saucepan over medium-low heat until butter melts and sugar dissolves, 2 to 4 minutes. Pour into greased baking dish and a layer of bread pieces over the top.

Beat milk, eggs, and vanilla extract in a bowl; pour milk mixture over bread. Press down or rearrange the pieces to make sure the bread is absorbing liquid. Sprinkle cinnamon over the top. Cover the dish with plastic wrap and refrigerate, 8 hours or overnight.

Preheat oven to 450 °. Remove plastic wrap from baking dish and sprinkle remaining brown sugar over the top of the bread mixture.

Bake in the preheated oven until browned and bubbling, about 30 minutes.

HAM 'N CHEESE EGG CUPS

These are a great low-carb breakfast option. You can add chopped spinach, bell peppers, or swap out the ham for sausage.

12 eggs
1/4 cup milk
1 cup diced ham
1 cup shredded cheese (your choice Swiss, cheddar, whatever)
1/4 cup chopped scallions (optional)
Salt and pepper

Preheat oven to 350°. Spray or grease muffin tin. Whisk together the eggs and milk. Stir in the ham, cheese and scallions, and a little salt and pepper if you like.
Use a soup ladle or ice cream scoop and fill each muffin cup. Bake for 15 to 20 minutes or until eggs are cooked. Remove egg cups from pan.

Gram Mae's Secret: *You can keep this in the fridge for 4 to 5 days or freeze them until ready to eat. Heat in the microwave 30 to 60 seconds if thawed or two minutes if frozen.*

PUMPKIN & PORK
FRENCH TOAST BAKE

Breakfasts in my house fall into two categories: quick and healthy or carbs, pork, and caffeine. Guess which this recipe falls into?

1 12 ounce package sweet breakfast sausage links
7 eggs
1 loaf French bread, cut in 1 inch cubes
2 1/2 cups milk
3/4 cup pumpkin puree
1/2 cup sugar
2 teaspoons vanilla extract
2 teaspoons pumpkin pie spice
Streusel Topping:
1/3 cup flour
1/2 cup brown sugar
1 teaspoon cinnamon
Pinch of salt
1/2 cup cold butter, cut into pieces

Spray or grease a 9 x 13 inch baking pan. Cook sausage according to package and cut into 1 inch pieces. In large bowl, whisk together eggs, milk, pumpkin puree, sugar, vanilla extract, and pumpkin pie spice.

In a very large bowl, combine bread, sausage and egg mixture. Stir until evenly coated with the egg mixture. Pour into baking pan. Cover casserole and refrigerate for several hours or overnight.

When ready to bake, use a fork to mix together flour, brown sugar, cinnamon, salt and butter until crumbly.

Preheat oven to 350°. Remove casserole from refrigerator and sprinkle streusel topping over the top. Bake loosely covered with foil for 40 to 50 minutes. Uncover and bake another 10 to 15 minutes. Let rest 5 to 10 minutes before serving.

Serve with warm syrup or whipped cream.

Sundays with Mae hadn't changed much since I was a little girl. Wake up before the sun, eat breakfast, and get to church before the good parking places were full. I found comfort in the predictable routine, even if it did involve getting up early and putting on pantyhose. Two things I hated more than lima beans and liver.

— *Twelve Spirits of Christmas*

SAUSAGE MUSHROOM QUICHE

Also known as Christmas Quiche. This recipe came from my best friend's mother, Nadia. I've served it on Christmas mornings for years. Use the make-ahead option, toss it in the oven when the kids wake up, and serve after the presents are opened.

1 9 inch frozen deep-dish pastry shell OR homemade
1 package 12 ounce bulk breakfast sausage
1 1/2 cups fresh mushrooms, sliced
1/4 cup onion, chopped
1/4 cup sweet red pepper, chopped
1/4 cup green pepper, chopped
1 3 ounce package cream cheese, softened
4 eggs
1/3 cup half and half cream
1 cup Monterey Jack cheese, shredded
1 cup cheddar cheese, shredded
1/4 teaspoon salt
1/4 teaspoon pepper
1 dash ground nutmeg

Bake pastry shell according to package directions or make your own; set aside. In a skillet, cook sausage over medium-high heat for 3 minutes, chopping into small pieces. Add the mushrooms, onion and peppers. Cook and stir 5 minutes longer or until sausage is no longer pink; drain and set aside.

In a large bowl, beat cream cheese until smooth. Beat in eggs and cream. Stir in the cheese, salt, pepper, nutmeg and the sausage mixture. Pour into pastry shell.

Bake at 350° 40 to 45 minutes or until a knife inserted near the center comes out clean. If necessary, cover edges of crust with foil to prevent over-browning. Let stand 10 minutes before serving.

Make ahead option: Bake pastry shell; cool on wire rack. Cover with plastic wrap and set aside. Prepare sausage and egg filling. Pour into a bowl; cover and refrigerate overnight. In the morning, pour filling into pastry shell and bake.

Aaron stepped forward and offered my mother his hand. "I hope you don't mind me tagging along. If your chicken is half as good as Mae's, how could I resist?"

Gram Mae choked on her sweet tea. "Of course, her chicken isn't as good as mine. She couldn't cook soup from a can."

— *Twelve Spirits of Christmas*

CHICKEN & TURKEY

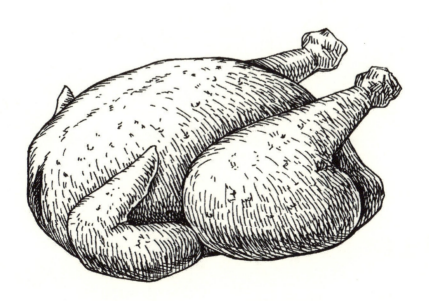

My great-grandmother patted the boy's shoulder. "You go right ahead. I'm sure Bryson won't mind if you say grace tonight."

"Dear Lord, thank you for the goulash and cornbread. Thank you for givin' us Jolene, and chocolate cake for dessert. Mostly, thank you for forgiving me for saying bad words and for Gram Mae not using the soap. In Jesus's name we pray. Amen."

"Amen." I'd given similar thanks a few times in my lifetime. Gram Mae might be a little old lady, but she ruled her house with a big stick and a bar of Ivory soap. — *The Spirit Child*

APRICOT GINGER CHICKEN

This delicious chicken can be grilled or oven baked. To grill, discard the marinade and shake excess liquid off the chicken before placing on a preheated grill. Cooking times will vary based on the kind of chicken you're cooking.

1 cup diced onion
1/4 cup fresh grated ginger
2 tablespoons olive oil
1/2 cup red-wine vinegar
2/3 cup soy sauce
1/4 teaspoon pepper
1 12 ounce jar apricot preserves
6 bone-in chicken breasts or 1 whole chicken cut up
Salt and pepper to taste

Soften onions and ginger in oil over low heat about 3 to 5 minutes. Stir in vinegar and boil 2 minutes. Add soy sauce, apricot preserves, and pepper. Simmer uncovered 2 minutes, stirring occasionally. Let cool 3-5 minutes. Pour sauce over chicken and marinate in the fridge 8 hours or overnight.

Preheat oven to 425°. Cover a shallow baking pan with foil or grease the dish. Arrange chicken and marinade in the pan in a single layer. Roast chicken until browned and cooked through 25 to 45 minutes total, depending on the type of chicken you're cooking.

Gram Mae's Secret: *Substitute 15-20 chicken wings and adjust cooking time for an appetizer.*

ARTICHOKE TOPPED CHICKEN & ROASTED POTATOES

An easy weeknight favorite, that tastes like you spent hours in the kitchen. It's the kind of dish I love to serve poolside with a glass of white wine.

5 small red potatoes
2 cups water
1 teaspoon salt
2 boneless, skinless chicken breasts (4-6 ounce)
1 teaspoon crushed rosemary
1 teaspoon lemon pepper
2 teaspoon olive oil, divided
1/2 cup chopped artichoke hearts
2 teaspoon chopped fresh parsley
4 tablespoons Parmesan cheese, divided in half
2 teaspoons mayonnaise

Preheat broiler on high. Cut potatoes into quarters. Place potatoes, water, and salt into pot and cook until tender. Drain and set aside.

For artichoke topping, place artichokes, parsley, 2 tablespoons of cheese, and mayonnaise in small bowl. Mix well.

Flatten chicken to 1/2 in. thickness using flat side of meat tenderizer. Sprinkle both sides of chicken with rosemary and lemon pepper.

In bowl, add remaining 1 teaspoon of the oil and remaining 1 teaspoon seasonings to potatoes; stir to coat.

Add 1 teaspoon of the oil to skillet; heat over medium-high heat 1-3 minutes or until shimmering. Place chicken and potatoes, cut side down, into skillet.

Cook 3-4 minutes or until chicken is golden brown. Turn chicken and potatoes over; cook an additional 3-4 minutes or until chicken is golden brown and centers are no longer pink.

Remove potatoes from skillet; set aside and keep warm. To finish chicken, spread artichoke topping evenly over chicken; sprinkle with reserved cheese.

Place on broiler pan as close as possible to heating element, 2 inches is ideal; broil 4-6 minutes until topping is golden brown and chicken is no longer pink. (Watch closely. If topping starts to brown unevenly, adjust accordingly.)

CAJUN BRINED TURKEY

Read this recipe to the end before attempting. It's not difficult, but it takes time and planning. They say patience is a virtue. In the case of this turkey, I have to agree.

For Cajun Mixture:
    2 tablespoons garlic powder
    2 tablespoons paprika
    1 tablespoon dried oregano
    1 tablespoon dried thyme
    1 tablespoon freshly ground black pepper
    1 tablespoon onion powder
    4 teaspoons cayenne pepper

For Turkey and Gravy
    6 quarts cold water
    1 cup kosher salt
    1 cup packed brown sugar
    2 rosemary sprigs
    One 14- to 16 pound turkey
    3 celery stalks, chopped
    2 green bell peppers, seeded, chopped
    2 yellow onions, chopped
    1/2 cup unsalted butter

Cajun spice mixture: Mix all the ingredients in small bowl. Brine the turkey: In a large pot, bring 1 quart of water to boil over high heat. Add salt, sugar, and 1/3 cup of the spice mixture. Stir until the sugar has dissolved. Add 1/2 rosemary. Remove from the heat and cool.

Pour the brine into a large container (5 gallons is best. I use the refrigerator drawer, but make sure the brine is cooled to room temperature before pouring into the plastic.) Add 5 quarts of cold water to the brine. Place the turkey into the brine, making sure it is entirely submerged. Cover the container tightly with plastic wrap and refrigerate for about 12 hours or overnight.

Roast the turkey

Roast the bird: Preheat the oven to 350°. Remove the turkey and rosemary from the brine. Discard the brine. Pat the turkey dry. Stuff the cavity with 1/2 the chopped celery, bell pepper, onion, and reserved brined rosemary sprigs. Tie the turkey legs together to keep the veggies in place.

In a small saucepan, melt 1/2 cup butter, remove from heat, and stir in 2 tablespoons of the spice mixture.

Place the remaining celery, bell pepper, and onion on the bottom of a large roasting pan. Place the roasting rack in the pan (over the veggies.) Next, set the turkey on the rack. Brush the spiced butter all over the turkey.

Cover the pan with aluminum foil and roast the turkey for 1 hour and 40 minutes. Baste the turkey and continue roasting uncovered for about 1 hour and 20 minutes longer, or until a meat thermometer reads 160°F when inserted into the part of the thigh nearest to the thigh and hip joint. Let turkey rest for 30 minutes before carving.

Gram Mae's Secret: *Serve with Oyster & Cornbread Stuffing for a New Orleans style holiday meal.*

CARIBBEAN CHICKEN

A summer favorite. Serve with pasta salad and fruit.

Juice of two limes or 4 tablespoons lime juice
1 tablespoon honey
1 tablespoon soy sauce
1 tablespoon olive oil
1 teaspoon minced garlic
1/2 teaspoon ground cumin
8 chicken thighs or other pieces with skin

In mixing bowl, stir lime juice, honey, soy sauce, olive oil, garlic, and cumin. Pour into a Ziploc bag, add chicken, coat chicken with the marinade. Squeeze out air, and seal the bag. Marinate in the refrigerator 1 hour or overnight.

Preheat an outdoor grill to medium-high heat For best results, spray the grate with cooking spray. Remove chicken thighs from the marinade. Shake to remove excess moisture. Discard remaining marinade.

Cook the chicken thighs until no longer pink at the bone and the juices run clear, about 6 to 8 minutes per side (more if grilling large chicken breasts.)

Gram Mae's Secret: *Substitute Jerk Seasoning for cumin for a Jamaican flavor. If cooking indoors, you can use boneless/skinless breasts. Bake in a 375° oven until done,* about 30 minutes.

CHICKEN CASSEROLE

In the south, neighbors are known to drop off casseroles when someone dies, has a baby, gets sick, moves in, is moving out, etcetera, etcetera. This is a quick and easy casserole that freezes well.

3 cups cooked shredded chicken meat (great use of leftovers)
2 cups chopped broccoli (thawed and drained if frozen)
1 can cream of chicken or cream of mushroom soup
1 cup sour cream or plain Greek yogurt
2 sleeves of Ritz crackers, crushed
1 stick butter, melted
2 tablespoons poppy seeds (optional)

Preheat oven to 350°. Lightly spray or grease a 3 quart baking dish. In a large bowl, mix the soup and the sour cream until well blended.

Add the shredded chicken and broccoli. Pour into prepared pan. Top with cracker crumbs and poppy seed.

Drizzle melted butter over the top of the crumbs. Bake 25-30 minutes or until crumbs are golden brown and casserole is hot and bubbly in the center.

CHICKEN AND DUMPLINGS

My kids could eat their body weight in chicken and dumplings! We absolutely love them, especially the little thick ones that fall to the bottom of the pan. They're almost as good as melted malted milk balls.

1 whole chicken
8 medium carrots, peeled and diced
2 cups frozen peas
For Dumplings
   2 cups plain flour
   3/4 cup water
   1/4 cup milk
   1/4 teaspoon salt
   1 teaspoon baking powder
   1 teaspoon shortening
Salt and pepper to taste

In a large stockpot, boil chicken until done and let cool. Save the broth! When the chicken cools, pick the meat from the bones. Strain the broth to remove any solids and skim off excess fat.

Bring the skimmed broth to a boil, add peas, and carrots. Salt and pepper to taste. Cover and simmer for 30 minutes, or until carrots are tender.

While carrots and chicken simmer, stir together dumpling ingredients until dough forms. Tear off grape-sized balls of dough and drop into boiling broth (or roll and cut dough into uniform dumplings if you prefer).

Stir as needed to ensure dumplings are submerged. Turn the chicken to medium low and simmer 10 minutes more.

"Tessa Marie, go get the big frying pan from Dottie's. I took out some chicken. We need to get dinner cooking before the boys come calling." Mae rubbed her hands together and took out flour, oil, and a dozen spices. Colonel Sanders didn't have a thing on Gram Mae.

— *The Spirit Tree*

CHICKEN ENCHILADA CASSEROLE

There's nothing healthy about this dish, but it will make your mouth happy. If you're looking for a heart-friendly recipe – swap the sour cream and soup with Greek style coconut yogurt seasoned to taste with taco seasoning.

2 tablespoons butter or olive oil
1 cup finely diced onion
1/2 cup finely diced green or red pepper (optional)
Salt and pepper
3 teaspoons cumin
3 to 4 boneless, skinless chicken breasts, cooked and shredded
2 cans cream of chicken soup
1 cup sour cream, plus extra for serving
2 cans diced green chilies
1 cup chicken stock
2 10 ounce cans enchilada sauce, split
4 cups Cheddar or Mexican Blend shredded cheese
18 small corn tortillas

Preheat oven to 350°. Heat butter or olive oil in a skillet. Add onions and peppers and cook on medium until the onions are translucent. Stir in cumin. In a large bowl whisk together canned soup, sour cream, stock, and green chilies. Stir in chicken and onions and peppers.

Pour 1 can of enchilada sauce into a 9 x 13 inch glass baking dish. Place a layer of tortillas on top of sauce, overlapping or cutting as necessary to form a solid layer. Cover tortillas evenly with 1/3 of the chicken mixture. Sprinkle 1/3 of the shredded cheese over chicken mixture.

Add another layer of tortillas. Pour, half of the second can of enchilada sauce over the tortillas. Add a layer of chicken mixture and then cheese.

Repeat process until you have 3 layers, ending with cheese layer. Bake covered loosely with foil for 20 to 25 minutes. Uncover and bake another 10 to 15 minutes or until cheese is melted and bubbly. Serve with extra sour cream on top.

My mother's voice rose to a pitch that rivalled a cat with its tail caught in a fan. "Tessa Marie, get your fanny over here. Dinner's getting cold. Nobody likes cold fried chicken."

"Actually, momma a lot of people like cold chicken." I'd always found it difficult to turn off my smart-mouth.

— *Twelve Spirits of Christmas*

CHICKEN MARSALA

This dish takes some time to prepare. It's best for a special supper. I played with the recipe over the years to get it right for my family's taste buds. I encourage you to do the same.

For the Chicken
    1 cup all-purpose flour, divided
    1 teaspoon salt
    4 large boneless, skinless chicken breasts
    3 tablespoons olive oil
    2 tablespoons unsalted butter
For the Marsala sauce:
    2 tablespoons unsalted butter, as needed
    1 pint (8 ounces) mushrooms, sliced
    2 cloves garlic, minced
    3/4 cup dry Marsala wine
    3/4 cup low-sodium chicken broth
    1/4 cup heavy cream
    Serving suggestions:
    Cooked pasta, such as angel hair
    Chopped fresh flat-leaf parsley leaves

Preheat oven 200°.
In a small bowl, mix flour and salt. Set aside.

Place one breast inside a gallon sized Ziploc bag. Pound with the flat side of a meat mallet or rolling pin to an even 1/4 inch thickness. Set the flattened chicken breast aside and repeat with remaining breasts.

Place the flour mixture inside the bag (make sure you haven't pounded any holes in it!) Add the flattened chicken.

Seal the bag and shake to coat.

Heat oil in a skillet over medium heat until shimmering. Add butter and swirl until melted. Add chicken in batches. Don't crowd the pan. Fry until golden-brown on both sides, 3 to 4 minutes per side. Remove the browned chicken to an ovenproof baking dish. Repeat with the remaining chicken breasts. Cover the chicken with aluminum foil and place in the oven to keep warm.

Keep the skillet heat on medium. Add up to 2 tablespoons more butter if the pan is dry. Add the mushrooms and cook until their juices start to release, about 3 minutes. Add the garlic and cook 1-2 minutes. Be careful not to burn the garlic. Add the Marsala and scrape the bottom of the pan to remove any browned pieces. Add the broth and simmer until reduced by half and it starts to thicken, about 15 minutes. Add the cream and return the chicken to the sauce. Cook until the sauce thickens and the chicken is well-coated, 3 to 5 minutes.

Serve over pasta or mashed potatoes. Garnish with chopped parsley and a squeeze of lemon.

CHICKEN PARMESAN

4 to 6 boneless chicken breasts

2 teaspoons garlic salt

1/2 teaspoon black pepper

2 eggs

1 tablespoon of water

1/2 cup flour

1 cup seasoned Italian bread crumbs

1/2 cup grated Parmesan, divided

3 tablespoons olive oil

1 jar (24 to 26 ounces) marinara sauce or homemade sauce

2 to 3 cups shredded mozzarella

Preheat oven to 375°. Pound out chicken to even out the thickness. (See Chicken Marsala recipe for instructions on pounding out chicken.) Season chicken with garlic salt and pepper.

In cake pan or shallow dish, whisk eggs and water together. Place flour in another dish. In a third dish, mix together the bread crumbs and 1/4 cup Parmesan cheese.

Heat oil to medium in a large skillet. Dredge the chicken in the flour. Next, dip them in the egg mixture. Last, place them in the bread crumbs and Parmesan and press until well coated.

Add the breaded chicken to the skillet and fry a few minutes on each side to brown it. Transfer chicken into a casserole dish that has been greased or sprayed with cooking spray.

Pour marinara sauce over chicken. Top with shredded mozzarella and the remaining 1/4 cup Parmesan cheese. Bake 20 to 35 minutes or until bubbly and the chicken is cooked through. Serve over pasta.

CHICKEN PIE

This is an old recipe from North Carolina. It's dryer than a traditional pot pie but very tasty. It's yummy served as is or with gravy.

Crust - Use the Perfect Pie Crust recipe on page 165.
Filling
    2 1/2 cups chopped cooked chicken
    1 teaspoon salt
    1 teaspoon ground pepper
    3 tablespoons flour
    1 cup chicken broth
    1-2 tablespoons butter, cut in pieces

Preheat oven to 375°. Roll out one piece of dough to form the bottom and sides of a 9 inch pie plate. Place in the plate. Roll out second piece of dough for top crust. Set aside.

Place chicken on bottom crust in pie plate. Sprinkle with salt, pepper, and flour, and pour in broth. Dot with butter. Cover with top crust, moisten edges with a little water and crimp to seal. Cut a few slits in top crust to allow steam to escape. (You can freeze unbaked pies.)

Place pie plate on a cookie sheet. Bake 45 minutes to 1 hour, until golden brown and bubbly. (If frozen, bake at 400° 1 to 1 1/2 hours.)

CHICKEN POT PIE

My kids love my chicken pot pie, and I like the versatility of this recipe. Use the easy method on weeknights or go full-on homemade on the weekends. Better yet, make a big batch and freeze the uncooked pies for a readymade dinner.

1/4 cup butter
1 small onion, chopped
3 celery ribs, chopped
3 carrots, chopped
2/3 cup peas
3 tablespoons chopped fresh parsley
1/4 teaspoon dried thyme
1/2 teaspoon poultry seasoning
1/4 cup all-purpose flour
1/4 cup butter
2/3 cup half-and-half cream
2 cups chicken broth
Salt and ground black pepper to taste
3 cups cooked chicken, cut into bite-size pieces
1 regular sized can refrigerated biscuits

Note - Use frozen "seasoning blend" chopped onions, peppers and celery to save time. Frozen peas & carrots can be substituted for fresh veggies. Cream of chicken soup can be substituted for flour, butter, and half-and-half. See Easy Method below.

Preheat oven to 350°. Melt butter in a skillet over medium-low heat, and cook the onion, celery, and carrots until the celery and carrots are tender, about 15 minutes, stirring occasionally. Stir in peas, parsley, thyme and flour, and cook, stirring constantly, until the flour coats the vegetables and begins to fry, about 5 minutes.

Whisk in chicken broth and half-and-half and cook until the sauce is thick and bubbling. Season to taste with salt and black pepper and mix in the chicken meat.

Easy Method – Mix frozen veggies, 1/2 cup water or milk and 1 can cream of chicken soup in mixing bowl. Add chicken. Transfer the chicken, vegetables, and sauce into a 2-quart baking dish. Arrange biscuits on top of the filling. Bake in the preheated oven until the biscuits are golden brown and the pie filling is bubbling, 20 to 25 minutes. Let rest 10 minutes before serving.

Variation - Purchase two pie shells. Instead of putting the chicken & veggie mixture into a baking pan, put it in one pie shell, then use the second to form the top crust. To do this, place the top crust over the filled pie, trim excess, and pinch the two crusts together along the edges. Use a fork to mash the pinched areas to make it look pretty. Cut a 1-2 inch slit in the top of the crust to allow it to vent. Bake at 350° one hour.

Gram Mae's Secret: *For recipes that call for cooked chicken, boil a whole chicken, cool, and pick the bones. Separate the meat into two freezer baggies with enough broth left over to cover the meat. Thaw the frozen chicken and both in the refrigerator OR put it in a pot and cook over medium heat until it's thawed. This will save you time when making paella, jambalaya, pot pies, etc.*

CHICKEN VESUVIO

This recipe is adapted from a dear friend's grandmother's not-so-secret recipe. It was his go to dish for dinner parties. The ingredients are simple but the flavor is out of this world.

1 whole chicken cut up
1/8 cup (approx.) dried oregano
Garlic powder
6 red potatoes cut into wedges
1 1/2 cups white wine
1 1/2 cups chicken stock
10 garlic cloves
1 bag frozen peas

Preheat oven to 375°. Season both sides of chicken pieces with salt, pepper, dried oregano and garlic powder. Coat large skillet with olive oil and brown potato wedges and chicken until browned. Remove from skillet and place in a roasting pan.

Place garlic cloves in the skillet and cook till golden. Deglaze skillet with the wine and add chicken broth. After it cooks down for five minutes pour wine mixture into the roasting pan. Bake for one hour and add frozen peas. Bake another 15 minutes or until chicken is cooked through.

CHICKEN AND YELLOW RICE

Simple home cooking. My youngest is a seriously picky eater, but he's been known to ask for seconds and thirds of this dish.

1 whole chicken
1 small onion, chopped and sautéed until soft
1 bag frozen peas & carrots
1 large package yellow rice
Salt and ground black pepper to taste

In a large stockpot, boil chicken until done and let cool. Save the broth! When the chicken cools, pick the meat from the bones. Strain the broth to remove any solids and skim off excess fat.

Measure broth to equal double the amount of liquid listed in the instructions on the rice package. If necessary, add water to achieve the correct amount of liquid. Bring the skimmed broth to a boil. Add yellow rice and bring to a boil. Add onion and peas & carrots to pot. Add chicken to pot and stir. Cover and simmer until the rice is done and the majority of the liquid is absorbed, 30-40 minutes. Salt and pepper to taste.

Note - Chicken broth will give the rice a richer flavor, but it also adds fat. Feel free to use water or store bought broth if this is too greasy.

Gram Mae's Secret: *If halving the recipe, put half the cooked chicken into a freezer baggie and cover with broth. Lay flat in freezer (Watch out for those pesky grate shelves, the bag will freeze AROUND the grate!) Frozen chicken can be used for pot pies, jambalaya, quesadillas, etc.*

MEXICAN CHICKEN

Easy peasy weeknight dinner.

1 pound boneless skinless chicken breasts, cut into 1/2 inch cubes
1 tablespoon vegetable oil
1 can whole kernel corn, drained
1 can tomato sauce
1 can chopped green chilies
1 1/2 teaspoons chili powder
1 teaspoon onion powder
Tortilla chips, soft tortillas, or hot cooked rice
Shredded cheddar cheese

In a large skillet, cook chicken in oil for 5-6 minutes or until no longer pink. Add corn, tomato sauce, chilies, chili powder and onion powder. Bring to a boil. Reduce heat; cover and simmer for 10-12 minutes, stirring occasionally. Serve over tortilla chips or rice and sprinkle with cheese.

ROASTED CHICKEN

Serve this with cornbread stuffing, mashed potatoes, and cranberry sauce for a taste of Thanksgiving anytime.

1 whole chicken
1-2 tablespoons olive oil, vegetable oil, or melted butter
Salt and black pepper
2 teaspoons Herbs de Provence
2 teaspoons Poultry Seasoning
Unsalted butter

Preheat the oven to 450°. Rinse the chicken, then dry with paper towels, inside and out. Salt and pepper the cavity, then truss the bird. (Google this, there are tons of techniques.) Rub chicken with oil. Salt the chicken (about 1 tablespoon). Season to taste with pepper, Herbs de Provence, and poultry seasoning. Place the chicken in a roasting pan and place on the center or lower rack in a preheated oven.

Roast chicken 15 minutes. Reduce the temperature to 350° and roast for 20 minutes per pound until it's done, 50 to 60 minutes. Remove from oven and baste the chicken with the pan drippings. Let it rest for 15 minutes before carving.

ROASTED CHICKEN PAN GRAVY

2 cups chicken stock
3 tablespoons flour
Sea salt and freshly ground black pepper to taste

Skim and discard excess fat from roasting pan. (You want the brown bits and the juices, not all the fat.) Place pan over moderate heat on top of stove (DO NOT do this with a glass pan.) Pour 1/2 cup of stock into pan and bring to a simmer. Use a spatula or flat whisk to loosen browned bits, for 1 minute. Transfer drippings to a heavy bottomed skillet.

In mixing bowl or coffee cup, blend flour with 1/4 cup of stock. Add to skillet. Set over moderate heat and cook, whisking constantly, until blended. Gradually add the remaining stock, stirring until mixture boils and thickens slightly, about 3 minutes. Add salt and pepper to taste.

SKILLET CORDON BLEU

Oooo-la-la, this recipe is delicious. Speaking French is optional.

4 boneless, skinless chicken breasts
Salt and pepper
3 tablespoons butter
1/2 cup white wine or chicken stock
1 can condensed cream of chicken soup
1 cup milk
8 thin slices of deli ham
1 cup shredded or sliced swiss cheese
1 tablespoon fresh chopped parsley

Season chicken with salt and pepper. Heat butter in a large skillet. Add chicken to the skillet and cook until brown on both sides and juices run clear.

Remove chicken and set aside. Add wine or stock to the pan. Increase the heat and bring to a simmer, loosening the brown bits from the pan. Add soup and milk. Whisk until smooth.

Return chicken to the pan. Top each piece with 2 slices of ham and 1/4 cup of cheese (or two slices). Cover skillet and cook for a few minutes until cheese melts. Garnish with parsley. Serve with egg noodles or rice.

SOUTHERN FRIED CHICKEN

I've been known to call my mom and ask her to make fried chicken for me. I don't know why, but mine never tastes as good as hers.

3 eggs
1/3 cup water
About 1 cup hot red pepper sauce (I use Texas Pete.)
2 cups self-rising flour
1 teaspoon pepper
1 whole chicken, cut into pieces
Oil, for frying
2 packets or one box Lipton Tomato Onion Soup Mix

Beat the eggs with the water in medium sized bowl. Add enough hot sauce to make the egg mixture the color of a carrot. In large bowl, combine the flour, pepper, and Tomato Onion Soup mix. Dredge chicken through the flour mixture, then dip in the egg mixture, and then coat a second time well in the flour mixture.

Heat the oil to 350° in a deep pot. Do not fill the pot more than 1/2 full with oil.
Fry the chicken in the oil until brown and crisp. Dark meat 13 to 14 minutes, white meat 8 to 10 minutes.

Gram Mae's Secret: *Preheat oven to 200°. Cook chicken in batches. Don't crowd the pan. When a piece is finished, set it on a paper towel a minute or two to drain the grease, then place it in a baking dish inside the warm oven until ready to serve.*

Finding food in Dottie's refrigerator reminded me of a game of hide-and-seek. All sorts of good things hid inside old plastic containers. The Cool Whip container held some potato salad—a keeper. I set it on the counter. The small Country Crock bowl contained green beans; those went back. The large Country Crock container held . . . margarine.

I opened an orange container and found leftover meat loaf. "Jackpot."—*The Spirit Tree*

STUFFED CHICKEN BREASTS

This is the most versatile chicken recipe ever!

2 tablespoons butter
1/4 cup finely diced onion
3 cloves garlic, minced
Salt and pepper
4 boneless, skinless chicken breast halves
3 to 4 tablespoons olive oil

Stuffing ideas – Pick one or create your own

Greek stuffing
    Juice from 1 lemon
    1/2 cup crumbled feta cheese
    4 teaspoons Greek Seasoning or Oregano
    1 box frozen chopped spinach, defrosted and squeezed dry

Italian stuffing

    4 teaspoons Italian seasoning
    1/2 cup mozzarella cheese
    1 can diced tomatoes or 1 cup marinara sauce
    1 package peperoni

Mini-Thanksgiving

    2 cups prepared stuffing or 1 cup stuffing 1 cup mashed potatoes
    1 cup cooked sage sausage
    1 can cranberry sauce (serve on the side)
    Gravy (serve on the side)

Prepare stuffing ingredients. Use common sense here. Cook any veggies until soft, otherwise, fill the pocket with a couple tablespoons of your ingredients.

Greek stuffing instructions

Heat butter in large skillet. Cook the onion in the butter for a few minutes until it starts to soften. Add garlic and cook another 30 seconds stirring constantly. Add the spinach, lemon zest, and a pinch of salt and pepper. Sauté a minute or two or until any liquid in the pan has evaporated and the spinach is dry. Remove from the heat, cool the mixture slightly, and stir in the feta cheese.

Lay chicken breasts on a flat surface. Use a knife to cut a pocket horizontally. Don't cut all the way through. Season chicken including the pocket with salt and pepper. Place a few tablespoons of the filling in the center of each breast. Secure pocket with a couple plain wooden toothpicks. You can wrap it with bacon if you really want to up the wow factor.

Place chicken in a baking dish and drizzle with olive oil and any desired seasoning (Italian, oregano, etc.) Bake in a pre-heated 400° oven for 35 to 45 minutes or until chicken is cooked through. Depending on the stuffing you choose, you can fry chicken breasts in a skillet with a few tablespoons of olive oil or grill chicken breasts about 5 to 7 minutes per side, flipping once until juices run clear and chicken is cooked through.

Gram Mae's Secret: *The sky is the limit with stuffing. Use your imagination. This is a great way to get rid of left overs. Just make sure the chicken is cooked through. Different fillings will impact cooking time.*

TURKEY SALTIMBOCCA

This is one of my daughter's favorite dishes. It looks fancy on the plate, but it's simple to put together. No turkey? It works great with chicken or pork.

4 four ounce turkey cutlets, about 1/4 inch thick
4 slices prosciutto or thinly sliced ham
2 tablespoons thinly sliced fresh sage
1 ounce Parmesan cheese
2 tablespoons all-purpose flour
2 tablespoons olive oil
3 tablespoons butter
1/2 cup chicken stock

If the cutlets are not of uniform thickness, flatten in freezer bag or between parchment paper using the smooth side of a meat mallet, to even them out.

Mix cheese with flour in small bowl. Heat olive oil in skillet over medium-high heat until shimmering.

Place a slice of prosciutto on each cutlet (tuck it in or fold it to match the shape of the cutlet. Place a sage leaf over prosciutto. Using flat toothpicks like straight pins, secure the sage leaves and prosciutto slices to the cutlets.
Dredge cutlet through the cheese mixture and sprinkle with sage.

Place the cutlets in the oil, sage and prosciutto side down and cook for 2-3 minutes, depending on the thickness of the cutlet. Turn them over and cook for 1-2 minutes. Remove to a warm plate and cover loosely.

Add broth and butter to pan. Stir to loosen the browned bits. Continue whisking until the butter is melted. Toss in any remaining cheese mixture and stir until bubbly. Remove the toothpicks from the cutlets. Spoon on the sauce.

WHITE CHICKEN CHILI

It doesn't get any easier than this. Toss in some chopped spinach or kale to turbo-charge the nutrients.

1 can or jar or cooked dried beans (48 ounces) great northern beans, drained
2 to 3 chicken breasts, cooked and diced or shredded
3 to 4 cups chicken stock
1 jar (16 ounces) thick and chunky green or red salsa
2 teaspoons cumin
Chili toppings: cheese, sour cream, onions, bacon, etc.

Dump it all in a large pot. Simmer 5 to 10 minutes, stirring often. Serve in bowls with your favorite chili fixin's on top. Serve with corn bread

Gram Mae's Secret: *This recipe can be made in a crock pot. Set to low for 4-6 hours. Raw chicken can be used but increase the cooking time. The longer it simmers the better it is.*

BEEF DINNERS

The kitchen smelled like heaven—if heaven served beef gravy and chocolate-chip cookies.

— *The Spirit Tree*

BEEF & BROCCOLI

A quick and easy weeknight dinner. Save time by using frozen broccoli and left-over meat. It's great with chicken and pork, too.

3 tablespoons cornstarch, divided
1/2 cup water, plus
2 tablespoons water, divided
1/2 teaspoon garlic powder
1 pound boneless round steak, 1 pound charcoal chuck steak, or chicken breast cut into thin 3 inch strips
2 tablespoons vegetable oil, divided
4 cups broccoli florets
1 small onion, cut into wedges
1/3 cup soy sauce
2 tablespoons brown sugar
1 teaspoon ground ginger
Hot cooked rice

Combine 2 tablespoons cornstarch, 2 tablespoons water and garlic powder until smooth. Add beef and stir to coat. Stir-fry beef in 1 tablespoon oil until beef reaches desired doneness over medium high heat in a large skillet or wok. Remove and keep warm. Stir-fry broccoli and onion in remaining oil for 4-5 minutes. Return beef to pan.

In small bowl, combine soy sauce, brown sugar, ginger and remaining cornstarch and water until smooth. Add to the pan. Cook and stir for 2 minutes. Serve over rice.

BEEF STROGANOFF

This is one of my personal favorites. Unfortunately, I rarely make it. One kid doesn't like mushrooms and another doesn't like sour cream.

2 pounds beef tenderloin or sirloin, cut into 1 inch pieces
Salt and pepper
1 cup flour
2 tablespoons olive oil
3 tablespoons butter
1 cup finely diced onion
8 ounces sliced mushrooms
1 tablespoon tomato paste
2 cups beef stock
2 cups cup sour cream
2 tablespoons cognac or dry white wine
Hot cooked egg noodles
3 tablespoons chopped parsley

Season beef well with salt and pepper. Lightly coat beef pieces in flour. In a large skillet, heat oil and quickly brown beef for a minute or two on both sides. Don't overcrowd the pan. Brown the beef in batches. Be sure to add more oil if the pan is dry. Remove beef from pan.

Add butter, onions, and mushrooms to the skillet. Cook until onions soften. Season with salt and pepper. Add tomato paste and beef stock. Bring to a boil. Be sure to scrape the brown bits from the pan.

Simmer 3-4 minutes, then turn the heat to low and stir in sour cream until smooth. Add cognac or white wine. Add beef back to skillet to reheat. Serve over warm egg noodles and garnish with parsley.

Note - If the sauce becomes too thick, add beef stock of milk a little at a time until it's the correct consistency.

HERB-ROASTED PRIME RIB

Forget the turkey, save the ham till New Year's Day. Serve prime rib and herbed mashed potatoes for a decadent holiday meal.

1 15 pound boneless rib roast
1 cup olive oil
1/4 cup fresh rosemary leaves
1/4 cup packed fresh sage leaves
1/4 cup fresh thyme leaves
2 tablespoons salt
2 tablespoons black pepper
5 cloves garlic, pressed

Preheat the oven to 500°. Put the rib roast in a large roasting pan and set aside for 30 minutes. Put the olive oil, rosemary, sage, thyme, salt, pepper and garlic in a food processor and pulse until everything is combined but not a paste. You want chunky herbs. Rub the mixture all over the roast. Roast for 20 minutes, then lower the oven temperature to 325°. Roast until the internal temperature registers 130° for medium rare, about 2 hours. Let rest for 10 to 15 minutes, then cut into 1/2 to 1 inch slices.

JALAPENO POPPER STUFFED MEATLOAF

What's better than a stuffed pepper? Meatloaf stuffed with a stuffed pepper AND wrapped in bacon! Warning: These are highly addictive.

1 cup bread crumbs
2/3 cup milk
2 pounds lean ground beef
2 tablespoons Montreal steak seasoning
2 tablespoons Worcestershire sauce
2 eggs, beaten
8 ounces cream cheese, softened
1/2 cup Monterey Jack Cheese, grated
6 small jalapenos
6 slices of bacon

Preheat oven to 375°. In a large bowl, mix together bread crumbs and milk. Let the milk absorb completely, then add ground beef, eggs, steak seasoning, Worcestershire sauce and eggs. Mix well and set aside. In a separate bowl, combine cream cheese and Monterey jack cheese. Boil jalapeno peppers to soften slightly. Watch out for the steam, it's filled with pepper juice and burns!

Stuff peppers with cheese mixture. Burry the stuffed jalapeno in a meatloaf ball, about the size of a human heart. Wrap the meatloaf ball with a slice of bacon. Bake 45 minutes until top is brown and meat reaches an internal temperature of 175°. Remove from oven and let rest 10 minutes before serving.

Gram Mae glanced up from the stove and narrowed her eyes. "Last time we had a family meeting, you burned your apartment down. Should I be worried?"

"Nothing's caught fire this time, I promise." I kissed her cheek and peeked into the pot. "Chicken and rice? Yum."

"Biscuits are in the oven." She hip-checked me when I reached for the spoon. "Set the table."
"Yes, ma'am." I grinned and pulled the soup bowls from the cupboard. "How was your day?"

Mae cast me a dubious look. "You sure nothing burned down?"

I laughed and set my hands on my hips. "I'm trying to be nice. Why do you assume the worst?"

"Because I know you." Gram Mae placed dinner on the table. —*Twelve Spirits of Christmas*

KOREAN BEEF BOWL

This is a versatile dish. Try different meat and veggie combinations.

2 green onions with tops, divided
1 pound cheap steaks
2 garlic cloves, pressed
3 tablespoons. soy sauce
1 tablespoons. sesame oil
1 teaspoon. coarsely ground black pepper
1 tablespoons. sugar
1 teaspoon. vegetable oil
Rice and vegetables
1 cup cooked rice
2 medium carrots
1 cup broccoli cooked.
2 cups bean sprouts

For the steak and marinade, slice the green onions and add to large mixing bowl. Cut the steak in thin slices against the grain. Add to the mixing bowl. Add the pressed garlic, soy sauce, sesame oil, black pepper and sugar and mix well. Cover, place in fridge at least an hour.

Peel carrots and discard skin. Use mandarin slicer or continue to peel carrots with potato peeler to make long ribbons. Alternatively, you can julienne slice the carrots. The shape doesn't matter, as long as they are thin. Place carrots in boiling water for 2-4 minutes. I like them crisp in this dish, but the kids prefer them soft.

To finish steak, add vegetable oil to skillet. Heat on medium-high heat 1-3 minutes or until shimmering. Add beef to skillet in a single layer and cook undisturbed 2 minutes or until beef is brown. Add broccoli and carrots. Stir, then cook an additional 3-4 minutes or until beef is no longer pink and veggies are warmed through. For rare or medium rare meat, warm vegetables before adding to the mixture. Remove from heat.

Place rice in individual serving bowls and spoon beef mixture on top. Garnish with reserved onion tops and bean sprouts.

Mae loved to play matchmaker almost as much as she loved to entertain. She pulled the leftover Salisbury steak from the night before. Unless I missed my mark, Mae planned shepherd's pie for dinner.

— *The Spirit Tree*

MEATLOAF

True confession time. This isn't my grandmother's meatloaf recipe—It's mine. I have to admit, I hate most meatloaf. Hate it with the all-consuming passion of a thousand suns. This recipe is simple and tasty. It doesn't have chunks of peppers and grease and gooey bits of Saltine crackers. If you like all that in your meatloaf, skip this one.

1 envelope Lipton® Recipe Secrets® Onion Soup Mix
2 pounds. ground beef
3/4 cup plain dry bread crumbs*
2 eggs
3/4 cup water
1/3 cup ketchup

Preheat oven to 350°. Combine all ingredients in large bowl. Shape into loaf in 13 x 9 inch baking or roasting pan. Bake uncovered 1 hour or until done. Let stand 10 minutes before serving.

Gram Mae's Secret: *Wondering what to do with the left over meatloaf? Use it to make shepherd's pie. Another option is to slice it up, dump gravy on top, and call it Salisbury Steak.*

ONE POT TURKEY CHILI MAC

1 1/2 pounds ground turkey
1 cup chopped onion
2 packets (1.25 ounces each) your favorite chili seasoning mix
2 1/2 cups water
1 can (14 ounces) petite diced tomatoes with green chilies
1 can (28 ounces) tomato sauce
2 1/2 cups uncooked elbow macaroni
1 can (16 ounces) chili beans (optional)
2 cups shredded cheddar cheese (optional)
2 to 3 tablespoons chopped scallions (optional)

In a large pot with a tight-fitting lid, brown ground turkey until crumbly and cooked through. Add onion and cook another few minutes. Add both packets of chili seasoning mix, water, diced tomatoes, tomato sauce, and macaroni. Bring to a boil.

Put lid on the pan and turn down heat. Simmer 10 to 18 minutes or until macaroni is tender, stirring occasionally. Uncover and stir in beans. Top with cheese. Turn off heat. Cover pan to let cheese melt.

Uncover and top with scallions if you like. Serve in bowls with your favorite chili fixin's on top like sour cream, crackers, and jalapeño peppers.

PEPPER STEAK

This is my best friend's recipe. I'll never forget the first time he made it for me. For some unholy reason, he dumped a quarter of a cup of oregano into the pan. Don't do this. It was awful.

1-2 pounds round steak
1/4 cup oil
2 large sweet yellow onions
2-4 green peppers
3-4 celery stalks (or bok choy)
3 tablespoons minced garlic
1 cup water
1/8 cup chives
1/4 cup soy sauce
1/4 cup teriyaki sauce
1/8 cup sugar
1/4 cup flour
2 beef bouillon cubes
Garlic Powder to taste
Ginger powder to taste
Black Pepper (course)

Brown meat in oil. Do not cook through. Take meat out of skillet, set aside. Add onions, peppers, and celery to the skillet. Cook until almost tender. Add seasonings. Add meat back into skillet. Mix water, sugar, and flour in a bowl. Add to skillet slowly. Bring to boil. Reduce heat to low and simmer 45-60 minutes. Serve over rice.

POT ROAST

I know I'm weird, but I love ketchup on my pot roast and gravy on my fries.

1 3 to 4 pound boneless beef chuck roast
4 teaspoons garlic salt
4 teaspoons black pepper
2 to 3 tablespoons olive oil
2 to 3 cups beef stock
1 cup dry red or white wine
1 large onion, chopped
4 to 6 stalks celery, cut into 2 inch pieces
6 to 8 cups potatoes and carrots, cut into 2 inch chunks
1/4 cup cold water
3 tablespoons all-purpose flour

Preheat the oven to 325°. Season meat with garlic salt and pepper. Heat 2 tablespoons oil in a large Dutch oven or skillet. Brown roast on all sides. Remove roast to a plate.

Add onion and celery to pan and cook for a minute or two. (Add more oil if needed.) Add beef stock and wine and bring to a boil. Loosen any brown bits in the bottom of the pan. Place roast back in the Dutch oven, or place roast in an ovenproof pan along with the stock and onion and celery.

Roast, covered, for 2 to 3 hours or until beef is fork tender. Place the extra vegetables around roast. Roast for another 50 to 60 minutes more or until meat and vegetables are tender. Place meat and vegetables on serving platter.

For gravy, whisk together cold water and flour until blended with no lumps; add the pan juices. Cook, whisking until thickened. Season with salt and pepper. If needed, add browning sauce if gravy is bland.

SHEPHERD'S PIE

I absolutely love shepherd's pie. I mean, who can you go wrong with mashed potatoes covered in cheese? I always make extra meatloaf and use the leftovers as my base for this yummy dish. Keep it simple and use store bought beef gravy instead of making the sauce.

For the potatoes
    2-3 pounds potatoes, peeled and chopped into 1 or 2 inch pieces
    1/2 cup salted butter
    1/4 cup sour cream
    1/4 cup milk, or to taste
    1 teaspoon salt
    1/2 teaspoon pepper
    1/2 teaspoon seasoning salt
    1/4 teaspoon garlic powder
    1/4 teaspoon onion powder

For the beef filling
    4 tablespoons (half stick) salted butter
    1 medium onion, chopped (about 2 cups)
    4-5 medium carrots, (about 1 and 1/2 to 2 cups)
    1 1/2 cups frozen peas
    1 1/2 pounds ground beef
    1 1/2 cups beef broth*
    1 tablespoon cornstarch
    1 1/2 teaspoons Worcestershire sauce
    1 teaspoon Better Than Bouillon paste* (see note)
    1 1/2 teaspoon salt, or to taste
    1/2 teaspoon pepper, or to taste
    1 cup shredded cheddar cheese

Preheat your oven to 350°. Add the chopped potatoes. Fill a large stock pot with enough water to cover potatoes. Cover and bring to a boil over high heat. Reduce to medium and continue boiling for 20-25 minutes, until the potatoes are fork tender. Drain return to the pot.

Add 1/2 cup butter. Mash with a potato masher until smooth. Leave chunks if you want. No judgement here. Stir in sour cream, milk, 1 teaspoon salt, 1/2 teaspoon pepper, seasoning salt, garlic powder, and onion powder. Cover and set aside. Note - seasonings are to taste. Adjust to suit your family's taste buds.

In large skillet, melt 4 tablespoons butter over medium heat. Add onions and carrots. Sauté 8 minutes, until the carrots are tender. Add ground beef. Break apart as it cooks until no longer pink. Drain the fat. Add the frozen peas.
In a small bowl, stir together beef broth, and cornstarch. Add this mixture to the meat, as well as the Worcestershire sauce. Cook over high heat 5 minutes, or until the mixture boils and the sauce has thickened. Cook and reduce until it has reached the consistency of gravy. Season with salt and pepper.

Pour the meat mixture into a deep 9x13 inch casserole dish. Top with the mashed potatoes and spread evenly. Top with cheddar cheese.

Bake 30 minutes, or until bubbly. Broil on the top rack 1-2 minutes to brown cheese.

SLOPPY JOES

This is a sweet recipe, if you prefer it spicy, omit the brown sugar and add 1/2 teaspoon smoked paprika, 1 teaspoon garlic powder, and 2 teaspoons red chili paste.

1 pound ground beef or turkey
1 small onion, chopped
pepper
1 tablespoon vinegar
1/2 teaspoon ground mustard
1/4 cup brown sugar
1/2 cup ketchup
hamburger bun

Brown ground beef and onion. Drain grease from beef and onion mixture. Return skillet with hamburger and onion to stove and add vinegar. Allow to evaporate. Add pepper and ground mustard and stir well. Add brown sugar and cook until hamburger is no longer pink. Add ketchup and simmer until mixture has thickened. Serve on hamburger buns.

STUFFED BEEF TENDERLOIN WITH RED PEPPER, SPINACH AND CHEESE

In my house, this is known as Harlin's beef tenderloin. I served it one year for Easter Dinner. While everyone was outside hunting eggs, Harlin, our Cocker Spaniel, ate the leftovers. I'm still not sure how a fifteen pound dog can put away five pounds of meat.

1 3 to 4 pound beef tenderloin, center cut
1 10 ounce package frozen chopped spinach, thawed and squeezed dry
1/2 cup crumbled feta cheese. White cheddar works if you're not a fan of feta.
1 small jar roasted red peppers, drained
Salt and freshly ground pepper
2 to 3 tablespoons olive oil

Dump roasted red peppers into a colander and place a heavy bowl or bowl of water on top of them to press out the moisture. These little buggers are tasty, but they can make this dish too drippy for my taste.

Butterfly the beef tenderloin by cutting the beef lengthwise down the center about two-thirds of the way through the beef. Open the beef tenderloin and pound the meat to 3/4 inch thickness. Season the flattened beef with salt and pepper.

Place the red peppers on top of the beef leaving a 1 inch border. Place the spinach and then cheese on top of the red peppers. Roll the beef up tightly, jelly roll fashion. Use butcher string to secure beef roll.

Preheat the oven to 375°. Drizzle roast with olive oil and season with a little more salt and pepper. Roast 30 to 40 minutes or until desired doneness. 135° for medium rare. Remove the stuffed beef tenderloin from the pan and allow to rest for at least 10 minutes before removing the string and slicing.

STUFFED PEPPERS

3 very large green bell peppers or about 5 small ones
1 15 ounce can tomato sauce
1/2 pound ground beef or turkey
1/3 cup chopped onion
1 cup cooked brown or white rice
1/8 teaspoon salt
1/8 teaspoon black pepper
1/8 teaspoon garlic powder
1 can tomato sauce

Preheat oven 350°. Cut the tops off the peppers and remove the seeds. Place the peppers in a large saucepan and cover with water. Bring to a simmer and cook 3 minutes, just until the peppers are slightly soft. Drain, rinse with cool water and set aside on paper towels to drain.

In a skillet, heat the ground beef and onion and cook until no pink remains. Drain. Add the salt, pepper, rice, garlic powder and half of the tomato sauce.

Stir well and spoon into the peppers. Top with the other half of the tomato sauce.

Bake in an ungreased dish 20 minutes. Cover with remaining tomato sauce and bake another 10-15 minutes. Serve warm.

Bryson smiled. "I'm a patient man."

Mae laughed and said, "Good. You'll need to be if you're going to marry my great-granddaughter. Now that we have that settled, eat before it gets cold."

— *The Spirit Tree*

STUFFED CABBAGE ROLLS

The sauce for this dish is amaze-balls, but if you're not into a sweet tomato sauce, omit the brown sugar, lemon juice, and cinnamon. Replace the traditional flavors with Italian seasoning or kick it up a notch and add taco or chili seasoning. Take a walk on the wild side while eating your veggies.

1 large cabbage, cored
1 (28 ounce) can crushed tomatoes, not drained
3 tablespoons light brown sugar
1/2 teaspoon cinnamon (my secret ingredient)
1 tablespoon Worcestershire sauce
1 tablespoon lemon juice
1 pound ground beef
1 cup cooked rice, cooled
1 small onion, chopped
1 egg
1 teaspoon salt
1/2 teaspoon black pepper

Preheat oven to 350°. Coat a 9 x 13 inch baking dish with cooking spray.

In a large saucepan, bring 1 inch of water to a boil over high heat. Place cabbage in water, cored-side down; cover pan, and reduce heat to low. Steam 20 minutes, or until cabbage leaves pull apart easily. Drain and set aside.

In a medium bowl, combine tomatoes and their juice, brown sugar, cinnamon, Worcestershire sauce and lemon juice; mix well and set aside. In a large bowl, combine ground beef, rice, onion, egg, salt, pepper, and 2 tablespoons tomato mixture; mix well.

Place 1 cup tomato mixture in bottom of prepared baking dish. Peel a cabbage leaf off the head and cut off thick stem. Place 1/4 cup meat mixture in center of leaf. Starting at core end, make a roll, folding over sides and rolling loosely. Place seam-side down in baking dish; repeat with remaining cabbage leaves and meat mixture. Spoon remaining tomato mixture evenly over top of cabbage rolls and cover.

Bake 1 1/4 hours. Uncover and cook 10 additional minutes, or until beef is no longer pink.

Gram Mae's Secret: *Instead of steaming the cabbage, an easy way to peel the leaves is to core the cabbage, freeze it overnight, thaw it completely, then peel away...easily! Don't stress if your leaves rip apart or are too small. Layer them until you have a large enough section to roll. No one will see the leaves under all that tomato sauce.*

TORTILLA CASSEROLE

My kiddos love this exactly as it's written. However, you can add layers of veggies, change the meat, or use whole beans instead of refried. Just be sure to use corn tortillas and enough liquid to keep everything moist.

Nonstick cooking spray or shortening
1 pound ground beef or turkey
1 packet taco seasoning
1 can chopped tomatoes, drained, with 1/3 cup juice reserved
1 can refried beans
1 1/2 cups frozen corn, thawed
8 corn tortillas cut into strips, 8 inch work great for this recipe
2 cups shredded Monterey Jack or cheddar cheese
1 jar of salsa
Sour cream (optional), for serving

Preheat the oven to 375°. Spray a 9 inch casserole/baking dish with nonstick cooking spray or grease it with shortening on a paper towel.

In large pan cook ground beef and onion until done. Drain well. Add the tomatoes with the 1/3 cup of reserved juice, salsa, corn, and the taco seasoning. Let simmer until everything is hot, about 3 minutes.

Coat bottom of baking dish with 1/2 cup meat mixture. Cover meat mixture with tortilla strips. Spread one third refried beans evenly over the tortillas, then sprinkle 1/2 cup of the shredded cheese evenly over the top.

Add another layer of tortilla strips. Followed by meat mixture and more tortillas. Repeat layers until all ingredients are used, ending with a layer of meat mixture and then the last 1/2 cup of shredded cheese.

Bake the tortilla casserole until it is hot throughout and the top is lightly browned, about 20 minutes. Let the casserole sit for about 5 minutes, then cut it into wedges using a sharp knife and serve it with a spatula.

Serve with sour cream and/or salsa on the side, if you like.

Gram Mae's Secret: *You can make the tortilla casserole a day ahead of time, cover it with plastic wrap or aluminum foil, and put it in the fridge overnight; just take it out and let it sit at room temperature for about 20 minutes while the oven preheats. Bake the casserole uncovered. You can also reheat the cooked casserole at 350° 15 to 20 minutes, until warm.*

PORK

My great-grandmother's voice came over the line and warmed my heart. "Tessa Marie, pick up an extra slab of ribs while your at the Walmart."

"We have two racks thawing. Are we having company?" I held my breath, praying she hadn't invited anyone awful to dinner.

"Darlene and her new beau stopped by. Hurry home, and don't you dare buy Halloween candy." She laughed and disconnected.

Gram Mae hadn't invited someone awful to dinner. She'd invited the queen of awful—my mother.

— *Twelve Spirits of Christmas*

AUTUMN FLAVORS PORK ROAST

3 to 4 pound boneless pork loin roast
2 to 3 cloves garlic, minced
Salt and pepper
1 can (16 ounces) whole berry cranberry sauce
1/4 cup brown sugar
3/4 cup apple juice
2 apples, peeled and chopped

Season roast with salt and pepper and rub garlic all over it. Place roast in the slow cooker.

In a bowl, whisk together cranberry sauce, brown sugar and juice. Pour it over the roast. Place the apples on top. Cover and cook on low for 8 hours or until tender.

Let rest 10 minutes before slicing. In the meantime, pour the sauce into a pan and simmer until it reduces and begins to thicken. Slice the roast and serve with the sauce.

CHEESY HAM AND HASH BROWN CASSEROLE

I'm a huge fan of breakfast for dinner. Add a side of scrambled eggs to this dish and you have a terrific breakfast – no matter the time of day.

1 26 ounce package frozen hash brown potatoes
1 pound ham steak, diced
1 can condensed cream of potato soup or cream of onion
1 cup shredded sharp Cheddar cheese
1/4 cup grated Parmesan cheese
Paprika

Preheat oven to 400°. Lightly grease a 9x13 inch baking dish.

In a large bowl, mix hash browns, ham, cream of potato soup, and 1/2 Cheddar cheese. Spread evenly into prepared dish. Sprinkle with Parmesan cheese.

Bake uncovered 25 minutes in the preheated oven, or until bubbly and lightly brown. Sprinkle with remaining cheese and paprika, bake another 5 minutes until cheese is melted. Serve immediately.

FLORIDA STYLE PORK CHOPS

These chops have a hint of island flavor, but less spice than traditional jerk pork.

1/2 cup orange marmalade
2 tablespoons orange juice
2 tablespoons Dijon mustard
1 tablespoon reduced-sodium soy sauce
1/2 teaspoon minced garlic
1/8 to 1/4 teaspoon crushed red pepper flakes
4 bone-in pork loin chops (1/2 inch thick about 8 ounces each)
1 teaspoon vegetable oil
1/2 teaspoon salt
1/4 teaspoon pepper

Combine the marmalade, orange juice, mustard, soy sauce, garlic and pepper flakes in a small bowl and set aside.

Season pork chops with salt and pepper, then brown both sides in oil in a large skillet. Continue to cook uncovered, 10 minutes longer or until a thermometer reads 160°. Remove and keep warm.

Add marmalade mixture to the skillet; bring to a boil. Reduce heat; simmer, uncovered 3-4 minutes or until thickened. Spoon over pork chops.

PEACHY PORK CHOPS

4 1 inch thick pork chops
1/4 teaspoon salt
1/4 teaspoon onion power
1 16 ounce can peaches, undrained or peach preserves
2 tablespoons brown sugar
2 tablespoons butter or margarine
1/2 teaspoon dried basil

Place pork chops on lightly greased rack of a broiler pan. Sprinkle with salt and onion powder. Broil 5 to 6 inches from heat, 7 minutes on each side.

Combine peaches and remaining ingredients in a saucepan. Cook uncovered on low 10 minutes, stirring often. Put pork chops on a platter and pour sauce over them.

SEAFOOD & FISH

"It smells good, Gram," I told her.

"Of course it does. Now put the chicken on the table, and one of you needs to explain why I was asked to plan a Bride Feast." Mae dried her hands and looked between us.

"Wait, wait. Don't tell yet. I want to hear this, too." Dottie came in with a basket full of tomatoes from the garden. Unlike Mae, Dottie seemed tickled by the newest turn of events.

I decided to let Bryson explain, since every time I opened my mouth, I put my foot in it. He shook his head and took his seat at the table—of all the times for him to be a coward.

"It's all a big misunderstanding," I said.
"Tessa Marie, I'm an old woman. I don't have all night to wait for you to tell me what happened.

I *know* it's a misunderstanding." Mae sat and passed the food.

I relayed the high points of our conversation with Buck. My life had more drama than one of their soap operas.

— *The Spirit Tree*

CRAB OR PLAIN CORN CHOWDER

6 slices bacon, cut in small pieces
1 cup finely diced onion
1/2 cup finely diced red bell pepper
3 tablespoons flour
1 tablespoon Old Bay
3 to 4 cups fresh corn of the cobb or frozen corn
1 can cream of celery soup
4 cups chicken stock
3 cups frozen southern style cubed hash brown potatoes, slightly thawed
1 1/2 cups heavy cream
Salt and pepper
1 small can crab meat or 1-2 cups
2 few tablespoons fresh chives or scallions (optional)

Cook bacon in a large soup pot until crisp. Remove bacon with slotted spoon and use paper towels to soak up grease. Drain all but 2 to 3 tablespoons of bacon drippings from the pot. Add onion to bacon drippings and sauté until softened. Add red pepper and cook until the pepper begins to soften. Add flour and Old Bay. Cook a minute or two stirring often.

Add stock and bring to a boil, whisking until it begins to thicken. Stir in cream of celery soup, potatoes, and corn and simmer for five minutes, stirring often. Add heavy cream and bacon and lower heat. Season with a little salt and pepper if needed. Turn off heat and top with crab meat. Cover and let sit for 5 minutes, before adding additional Serve with chopped chives or scallions on top if you like.

CRAWFISH ETOUFFEE

If crawfish are hard to come by in your neck of the woods, shrimp works in this recipe, too. Come to think of it, you could use chicken or just about any meat in Etoufee, just don't tell Paul Prudhomme I said so.

3 cups long grain white rice
6 cups water
3/4 cup butter
1 large onion, chopped
3 stalks celery
1 clove garlic, chopped
1/4 cup all-purpose flour
1 pound crawfish tails
2 tablespoons canned tomato sauce
1 cup water, or as needed
6 green onions, chopped
salt and pepper to taste
1 1/2 tablespoons Cajun seasoning, or Old Bay

Combine the rice and water in a saucepan and bring to a boil. Cover, and reduce heat to low. Simmer for 15 to 20 minutes, until rice is tender and water has been absorbed.

While the rice is cooking, melt the butter in a large skillet over medium heat. Add the onion, and sauté until transparent. Stir in the garlic and cook for a minute. Stir in the flour until well blended. Gradually stir in the tomato sauce and water, then add the crawfish tails and bring to a simmer. Add the green onions and season with salt, pepper, and Cajun seasoning. Simmer for 5 to 10 minutes over low heat, until the crawfish is cooked but not tough. Serve over hot cooked rice.

HOT-HAVANA PAELLA

If you read the jambalaya recipe above, this will look real familiar. Modern Southern cooking is about playing with basic recipes and creating new flavor combinations.

1/2 pound shrimp, peeled and deveined
1 pound chicken breast cut into bite-sized chunks
1/2 pound chorizo or other spicy sausage OR diced ham OR whatever leftover meat you have in the fridge
2 tablespoons extra-virgin olive oil
2 cloves garlic
1 onion diced
2 cans (14 ounce) stewed tomatoes undrained
1 cup peas & carrots
1 10 ounce package of yellow rice
1 cup water (may need more. You can also substitute chicken stock)
1/2 teaspoon dried oregano
1/2 teaspoon cumin

Place the olive oil in a large pot (with lid) and heat the oil until hot. Brown chicken and other uncooked meat over medium heat. Add garlic and onion. Cook, stirring constantly, 5 minutes or until meat is done. Stir in tomatoes, rice, water, peas & carrots, other fully cooked meat and seasonings. Bring to boil, cover and reduce heat to simmer for 25 minutes.

Add shrimp. Cover and simmer 5 additional minutes.

Note - You may need to add more water before the rice is done.

JAMBALAYA
aka "Yaya"

Okay, y'all. Here's the thing. I can't give you my personal jambalaya recipe. If I did, my kids would never come home for Sunday supper. Plus, it takes days to cook right, and I've never actually measured the ingredients. So, here's a quick and easy one to get you rockin' and rollin' New Orleans style.

1/2 pound shrimp, peeled and deveined
1 pound chicken breast cut into bite-sized chunks
1/2 pound andouille or other spicy sausage OR diced ham OR whatever leftover meat you have in the fridge
2 tablespoons extra-virgin olive oil
3 tablespoons butter
2 cloves garlic
1 onion diced
2 bell peppers diced
1 cup celery diced
2 cans (14 ounce) stewed tomatoes undrained
1 can tomato sauce
1 10 ounce package of yellow rice
1 cup water (may need more. You can also substitute chicken stock)
1 tablespoon Old Bay

Place the olive oil in a large pot (with lid) and heat the oil until hot. Brown chicken and other uncooked meat over medium heat. Add butter, garlic, onion, peppers, and celery. Cook, stirring constantly, 5 minutes or until meat is done.

Stir in tomatoes, rice, water, peas & carrots, other fully cooked meat and seasonings. Bring to boil, cover and reduce heat to simmer for 25 minutes **Note** - you may need to add more water before the rice is done.) Add shrimp. Cover and simmer 5 additional minutes.

Gram Mae's Secret: *You can love to soak in a hot bath, and you can love shrimp, but shrimp don't love to sit in a tub. They prefer to steam. Place them on top of your hot food, cover, and turn off the heat. They'll cook through in about 5 minutes and not turn to rubber.*

N'AWLINS STYLE SHRIMP & GRITS

My friends from the low-country in Georgia swear by a cream sauce for Shrimp and Grits. I'm more of a tomato-based sauce girl myself. Except in clam chowder, then I'm all about the cream. Seriously, those folks in Manhattan do a lot of things right, but clam chowder isn't one of them.

1/3 cup green hot pepper sauce
1/4 cup dry white wine
1 shallot, chopped
1 tablespoon fresh lemon juice
1 tablespoon rice vinegar
1 cup whipping cream
5 cups water
3 cups whole milk
1/4 cup (1/2 stick) unsalted butter
2 cups grits
1/4 cup olive oil
8 ounces smoked andouille sausage, sliced. Other sausage works, but andouille is the gold standard for this dish.
1 red bell pepper, chopped
1 yellow bell pepper, chopped
1/2 cup minced onion
4 garlic cloves, chopped
30 uncooked large shrimp, peeled, deveined
4 plum tomatoes, chopped
2 teaspoons Cajun seasoning or Old Bay seasoning

Combine hot pepper sauce, wine, shallot, lemon juice and vinegar in heavy medium saucepan. Boil over medium heat until reduced to 1/2 cup, about 15 minutes. Stir in 1/2 cup cream.

For grits.

Bring 1/2 cup cream, 5 cups water, milk and butter to simmer in heavy medium saucepan. Gradually whisk in grits. Simmer until grits are very soft and thickened, stirring frequently, about 1 hour.

Note - This cooking time may be drastically different depending upon the type of grits used. I prefer a heartier corn grit or polenta. Follow liquid requirements and cooking time on grit package for best results.

For shrimp.

Heat olive oil in heavy medium skillet over medium heat. Add sausage, both bell peppers, onion and garlic; sauté until vegetables are tender, about 8 minutes. Add tomatoes, Cajun seasoning or Old Bay seasoning and sauté about 6 minutes. Turn off the heat and add shrimp. Cover and let sit 5 minutes or until shrimp are pink throughout. Season to taste with salt and pepper.

To finish.

Bring hot pepper-cream sauce to simmer. Spoon grits onto 6 plates, dividing equally. Spoon shrimp mixture over grits. Drizzle hot pepper-cream sauce over and serve.

PAN FRIED LEMON PEPPER FISH

I'm not a fan of fresh water fish. Which is a huge problem living in an area surrounded by lakes and rivers. Growing up, we had fresh caught fish at least once a week. The lemon pepper and onions in this recipe cut down the "fish" taste enough for me to enjoy it.

2 fish fillets (I prefer white flaky fish, but other varieties work, too.)
1 onion, sliced
1 teaspoon dried dill
2 tablespoons melted butter
2 teaspoons fresh lemon juice
1 lemon

Preheat oven to 400°. Cut 4 thin lemon slices. Place slices in the bottom of a baking dish. Place the fish fillets on top of the lemon slices. Season each piece of fish with salt, pepper and dill and then drizzle fresh lemon juice.

Place onion slices on top of fish and drizzle with melted butter. Bake for 15 to 25 minutes or until fish is white and flaky. Serve with fresh lemon slices.

SHRIMP CREOLE

Hands down, the best Shrimp Creole I've ever eaten is Antoine's in the French Quarter. It's buttery. It's spicy. It's succulent. It's approximately $2.50 per bite! This recipe is considerably cheaper, and you don't have to be in NOLA to enjoy it. However, if you ever find yourself in New Orleans, be sure to dine at Antoine's. On a budget? Go for lunch!

2 tablespoons olive oil
4 garlic cloves, minced
2 large onions, chopped
2 stalks celery, chopped
1 green bell pepper, chopped
1 teaspoon cayenne pepper
2 cups seafood stock or shrimp stock
1 (28 ounce) can whole tomatoes, in thick puree
Dash Worcestershire sauce
Dash hot sauce
2 bay leaves
Kosher salt and freshly ground black pepper
2 pounds large shrimp (about 32), shelled and deveined
4 tablespoons green onions, sliced for garnish

Heat a large heavy Dutch oven over medium heat. Add oil. Add garlic, onions, celery, and green bell peppers. Cook until softened, about 5 minutes. Stir in cayenne and let caramelize. Add the seafood stock, tomatoes, Worcestershire, hot sauce, and bay leaves. Season with salt and pepper. Simmer for 35 minutes.

Add shrimp, cover, and turn the heat off. Let stand about 5 minutes, until the shrimp are bright pink and cooked through. Garnish with green onions.

SHRIMP & ORZO

1 pound large uncooked shrimp
1 tablespoons (15 mL) vegetable oil
1/4 teaspoon (1 mL) salt
1/4 teaspoon (1 mL) coarsely ground black pepper
1/8 teaspoon (0.5 mL) sugar (see Cook's Tip)
8 ounce orzo pasta
1 garlic clove, pressed
2 cups chicken or seafood broth
1 cup clam juice
1 lemon
1 cup frozen peas
1 tablespoon butter

Peel and devein shrimp. Add oil to pan. Heat over medium-high heat 1-3 minutes or until shimmering. As pan heats, combine salt, black pepper and sugar in small mixing bowl. Add shrimp and toss to coat.

Arrange shrimp in a single layer in pan and cook about 1 minute or until one side is browned and edges are pink. Remove pan from heat and turn shrimp over. Let stand an additional 30 seconds or until centers are opaque and shrimp is cooked through. Remove shrimp from pan and set aside.

In same pan, combine orzo, pressed garlic, broth and clam juice. Bring to a boil. Cover and reduce heat to medium-low. Cook 10-12 minutes or until orzo is cooked through. As orzo cooks, zest lemon. You'll need 1 tablespoon zest and 1 tablespoon juice.

Remove Skillet from heat and stir in peas, butter and lemon juice. Arrange shrimp over orzo; cover and let stand 3-5 minutes or until heated through. Sprinkle with lemon zest.

My Aunt Dottie motioned to the mountain of tin foil covered dishes. "Selma, from next door, brought over Tuna Surprise, and some of the ladies from the church showed up with more food. We'll be eating sympathy casseroles for weeks."

Neither my aunt nor my great-grandmother cared for other people's cooking. Dinners would be like eating with a couple of food critics.

— *The Spirit Tree*

TUNA CASSEROLE

2 tablespoons butter
1 cup finely diced onion
1 cup finely diced celery
1 teaspoon garlic salt
2 cans (10.75 ounces each) cream of mushroom soup
1 3/4 cups milk
1/4 cup dry white wine (optional)
1 cup frozen peas
2 cans (5 ounces each) albacore tuna packed in water, drained
3 cups shredded cheddar cheese
2 cups crushed potato chips or crushed croutons
1 pkg. (16 ounces) egg or shell shaped noodles, cooked al dente

Preheat oven to 350°. In a large pan melt the butter. Cook onion and celery in the butter until the vegetables start to get soft. Season with garlic salt and pepper.

Add mushroom soup, milk and wine. Stir and heat until smooth. Add tuna, noodles and peas. Stir and coat with the sauce.

Spoon into a 9 x 13 inch baking dish that has been sprayed with cooking spray and top with cheese and potato chips or croutons. Bake for 30 to 45 minutes until bubbly and golden.

PASTA

Once he took the first bite, he inhaled the remainder of the bowl and three biscuits.

I enjoyed watching him eat, knowing in some small way I'd taken care of him. The feeling surprised me on many levels. I'd never considered myself the domestic type.

— *Twelve Spirits of Christmas*

HAM & SPINACH TORTELLINI

1 package refrigerated cheese-filled tortellini
1 package fresh baby spinach leaves (about 8 cups)
1 8 ounce cooked ham steak, diced
1 large red bell pepper
1/4 cup butter (NO margarine)
Coarsely ground black pepper

Cook tortellini according to package directions. As tortellini cook, place spinach into large colander, set in sink. Drain tortellini over spinach in colander.

Heat skillet to medium and add butter. Cook until the butter is a deep brown 5-7 minutes, swirl pan occasionally. Immediately add bell pepper. Reduce heat to low; add ham, tortellini and spinach. Gently toss to coat.

OLD-FASHIONED ITALIAN MEAT SAUCE

2 pounds lean ground beef
1 pound ground pork or bulk Italian Sausage
2 tablespoons olive oil
2 onions, chopped
1 clove garlic, crushed
3 cups red wine
2 pounds fresh mushrooms, sliced
1/4 teaspoon dried rosemary
4 tablespoons chopped fresh oregano
1/4 teaspoon chopped fresh thyme
3 (29 ounce) cans tomato sauce
1 (6 ounce) can tomato paste
2 tablespoons grated Parmesan cheese

In a large skillet, brown beef and pork over medium heat until no longer pink. Set aside.

In a large skillet, warm olive oil over medium heat and sauté onions and garlic until tender; add about 1/2 cup of wine. Mix well.

Add mushrooms, rosemary, oregano and thyme to skillet and add another 1/2 cup wine; sauté until tender.
Add browned meat, tomato sauce and tomato paste to mixture; simmer for 1 hour and add the remaining 2 cups of wine.

Simmer sauce on low for 2 to 3 hours, stirring occasionally.

Gram Mae's Secret: *Sauce can be portioned out and frozen in plastic containers.*

RAVIOLI LASAGNA

1 pound ground beef
1 tablespoon chopped garlic
1 teaspoon garlic powder
1 teaspoon salt
1/2 teaspoon ground black pepper
2 (24 ounce) jars prepared pasta sauce
1 teaspoon Italian seasoning
1 teaspoon dried basil
1 teaspoon dried oregano
1 (25 ounce) package frozen cheese ravioli
2 cups shredded mozzarella cheese

Directions for Slow Cooker
Heat a large skillet over medium-high heat. Cook and stir beef, garlic, garlic powder, salt, and pepper in the hot skillet until meat is browned and crumbly, 5 to 7 minutes. Drain and discard grease. Stir pasta sauce, Italian seasoning, basil, and oregano into ground beef mixture.

Ladle a generous layer of meat sauce into the bottom of a slow cooker; add a layer of ravioli. Ladle another layer of meat sauce over ravioli layer; alternate with remaining ravioli and meat sauce until all ingredients are used.

Cook on Low for 3 to 5 hours. Sprinkle ravioli mixture with mozzarella cheese and continue cooking until cheese is melted, 45 minutes to 1 hour more.

Directions for Oven
In a greased 2-1/2-qt. baking dish, layer a third of the meat sauce, half of the ravioli, and 1/2 cup cheese; repeat layers. Top with remaining sauce and cheese.
Cover and bake at 400° 40-45 minutes or until heated through.

SKILLET LASAGNA

1 jar (24-26 ounce) marinara sauce
3 cups water
8 ounce lasagna noodles
1 pound bulk hot Italian turkey sausage or sausage links, casings removed
2 garlic cloves, pressed
2 ounce Parmesan cheese
2 tablespoons chopped fresh parsley, divided
1 cup fresh whole milk ricotta cheese
1/2 cup shredded mozzarella cheese
1/4 teaspoon coarsely ground black pepper
Additional grated Parmesan cheese (optional)

Combine sauce and water in skillet. Cover and bring to a boil.

Break noodles crosswise into quarters. Stir noodles into sauce. Cover and reduce heat and simmer 16-18 minutes or until noodles are tender, stirring occasionally.

As noodles cook, place sausage into skillet; cook and stir over medium-high heat 6-8 minutes or until sausage is no longer pink, breaking into crumbles. Add pressed garlic. Cook 1 minute. Remove from heat. Stir sausage into noodles and sauce.

Grate Parmesan cheese. Chop parsley and set aside 1 tablespoons parsley for garnish. Combine cheeses, remaining parsley and black pepper in medium sized bowl. Scoop cheese mixture over noodles. Cover skillet and simmer gently 3-5 minutes or until cheese is melted and ricotta mixture is heated through. To serve, sprinkle lasagna with reserved parsley and additional Parmesan cheese, if desired.

SPINACH RAVIOLI CASSEROLE

1 jar (24 to 26 ounces) marinara sauce
1 1/4 cups water
1 package (24 ounces) frozen beef or cheese ravioli
3 to 4 cups shredded mozzarella cheese
1 box frozen chopped spinach, thawed and squeezed dry
1/4 cup grated Parmesan cheese

Mix marinara sauce and water together in a large bowl. Spoon half the sauce into a 9 x 13 casserole dish that has been sprayed with cooking spray. Top with half of the ravioli, mozzarella cheese, and spinach. Repeat layer. Top with Parmesan cheese.
Bake uncovered, at 350° 25 to 40 minutes or hot and bubbly.

I appreciated Dottie's effort to turn the conversation, but Darlene watched me from across the table. I recognized the look from when she'd tried to quit smoking. She wanted those ribs as much as her body wanted nicotine.

— *Twelve Spirits of Christmas*

STUFFED MANICOTTI

12 large manicotti
4 cups shredded mozzarella cheese, divided
2 cups ricotta cheese
6 tablespoons chopped fresh basil or 2 tablespoons dried basil
26 ounces spaghetti jarred or homemade sauce, divided
1/2cup grated parmesan cheese or 1/2 cup Romano cheese

Preheat oven to 350°. Spray 13x9 inch baking dish with nonstick cooking spray.

Cook pasta according to package directions, but DON'T OVERCOOK. Shoot for al dente. Carefully remove each shell and rinse with cool water. Let pasta dry on paper towels. Don't get too upset if a couple break, it's bound to happen.

In a large Ziploc bag, put in 3 cups mozzarella with the ricotta and fresh basil. Seal the bag tightly. Kneed the bag until the ingredients are thoroughly mixed. Cut the bottom corner of the Ziploc bag. Be sure the hole is smaller than the manicotti. Squeeze the cheese mixture into each manicotti. Spoon 2 cups spaghetti sauce into prepared baking dish.

Arrange stuffed pasta over sauce. Pour remaining spaghetti sauce over top of pasta. Sprinkle with remaining mozzarella and parmesan cheeses. Bake manicotti for 25 minutes.

SIDES & SNACKS

Dottie sighed. "We put salt pork in the greens. There's bacon in the green beans and potato salad. Darlene didn't tell us you were a vegetarian."

Mae wiped sauce from her fingers. "What's a vegan?"

Bryson chuckled. "He's a vegetarian who doesn't eat any dairy or eggs."

"Well, what the heck is left?" She smirked and added a few more ribs to her plate.

— *Twelve Spirits of Christmas*

BACON-OYSTER BALLS

1/2 cup herb seasoned stuffing mix
1 5 ounce can oysters, drained and chopped
1/2 cup finely diced onion
1 tablespoon minced garlic
1/4 cup water
8 slices of bacon, lightly cooked and cut in half

Preheat oven to 350°. Combine stuffing mix, oysters, onion, garlic, & water. Form into tablespoon sized balls. Wrap a half slice of bacon around each ball and secure with a wooden toothpick. Place on rack in baking pan. Bake for 25-30 minutes.

BACON WRAPPED BREADSTICKS

24 sticks sesame breadsticks, (1 package), 4 1/2" long
12 slices bacon
2 teaspoons garlic salt, or garlic powder
1 cup Parmesan cheese, grated

Preheat oven to 350°. In a mixing bowl, combine the Parmesan cheese with garlic salt and set aside. Cut the bacon slices in half so they are approximately 5 inches long.

Wrap each bread stick with one slice of bacon, starting at one end and ending at the other. Place wrapped bread sticks on a cookie sheet lined with parchment paper, and bake for 15 minutes or until bacon is browned.

Remove from oven and immediately roll bread sticks in cheese mixture. Let cool and serve at room temperature. Makes 2 dozen breadsticks.

BRANDIED SWEET POTATOES

2 pounds sweet potatoes, peeled and diced
1/2 cup butter
1/2 cup packed brown sugar
1/2 cup brandy
1/2 teaspoon salt

Place sweet potatoes in a large saucepan with enough water to cover. Bring to a boil. Cook 15 minutes, or until tender but firm. Drain, and set aside.

In a large skillet over low heat, melt the butter. Stir in the brown sugar, brandy, and salt. Add the sweet potatoes, and stir to coat. Cook, stirring gently, until sweet potatoes are heated through and well glazed.

BUFFALO WING DIP

I first tasted this dip at a neighborhood block party. My amazing next-door neighbor, Tammy, brought this dish. It was love at first bite.

10 ounce chicken
1 8 ounce package of cream cheese
1/2 cup wing sauce
1/2 cup ranch dressing
2 cups Monterrey jack cheese

Spread cream cheese in the bottom of a shallow (glass) baking dish. Spread chicken over cream cheese. Drizzle wing sauce over chicken. Drizzle ranch dressing over wing sauce. Sprinkle cheese on top. Bake at 350° 22 – 25 minutes.

Note - DON'T mix the liquids!

Gram Mae walked down the porch steps with enough banana pudding to serve two counties. "It's as wrong as hot pants in Sunday service. Men don't belong at baby showers."

— *The Spirit Child*

CHUCKY-CHEESE-HEAD MAC N' CHEESE

When my oldest was little, he loved to go to Chucky Cheese but pronounced the name of the restaurant Chunky-Cheese-Head. I have no idea where the "head" came from but I strongly suspect his great-grandfather had something to do with it.

4 tablespoons butter
1/2 cup finely diced onion
2 cloves garlic, minced
4 tablespoons flour
1 bottle (12 ounces) beer
2 1/2 cups milk
5 cups shredded cheddar cheese, divided
1 tablespoon Dijon mustard
1 teaspoon garlic salt
1/4 teaspoon black pepper
2 dashes hot sauce
1 box (16 ounces) elbow macaroni, cooked al dente
1 pound of bacon, cooked and crumbled (optional)
1/4 cup grated Parmesan cheese
1 cup crushed pretzels or 1/2 cup seasoned Italian breadcrumbs

Melt butter in a large non-stick pan. Cook onion in butter over medium heat until soft. Add garlic and cook another 30 seconds. Whisk in flour, stirring for a minute or two until well combined. Add beer and milk, whisking constantly. Bring to a boil. When it starts to thicken, turn down heat. Add mustard, garlic salt, pepper and 3 cups of cheese a handful at a time. Whisk until cheese is melted. Add hot sauce and bacon. Pour cheese mixture over cooked noddles.

Place cheesy noodles into a casserole dish. Mix crushed pretzels or breadcrumbs and parmesan cheese in small bowl. Sprinkle over top of noodles.

Bake in a 350 oven until bubbly, about 40 minutes.

CRANBERRY-PINEAPPLE GELATIN MOLDS

These were my gramma's favorite holiday dish. They're sweet and tart, and a nice contrast to stuffing and mashed potatoes.

24 paper or foil muffin liners (I prefer foil because they are easier to remove)
1 can (20 ounce.) crushed Pineapple, in juice, undrained
2 pkg. (0.3 ounce. each) Raspberry gelatin
1 can (16 ounce.) whole berry cranberry sauce
2/3 cup chopped walnuts
1 apple, chopped

Drain pineapple and save the juice. Add enough water to juice to measure 2-1/2 cups total liquid. Pour into saucepan and bring to a boil. Place gelatin in large bowl and add boiling juice/water. Stir until completely dissolved.

Stir in pineapple, cranberry sauce, nuts and apples. Spoon into 24 paper or foil-lined muffin cups. Refrigerate 2-1/2 hours or until firm. Remove from liners before serving.

DILLED CUCUMBER FINGER SAND-WICHES

1 3 ounce package cream cheese
1 tablespoon milk
1/2 teaspoon dried dill weed
1/4 teaspoon onion juice (you read that right. Juice an onion)
Dash of salt
6 slices white bread (Pepperidge farm fancy white or something similar. Think fancy.)
1 cucumber, thinly sliced
Beat together cream cheese, milk, dill, onion juice, and salt. Trim crusts from bread. Spread 1 tablespoon cheese mixture on each slice of bread. Cut into triangles. Top each with cucumber slices.

My men joined me, each with a plate overflowing with food. With a pang of jealousy for their metabolisms, I shoveled a bite of lettuce into my mouth. Life wasn't fair.

— *The Spirit Child*

FRIED CREAM CORN

12 ears fresh corn, shucked
4 slices thick slab bacon
1/2 stick butter
Freshly ground black pepper

Remove corn from cobs and mash the whole kernels slightly. Slice bacon into 1 inch pieces. Cook bacon until brown in a large skillet. Remove bacon from skillet and add 1/2 stick butter to bacon grease. Over medium-high heat, pour in the corn. Fry in the grease and butter mixture. Lower the temperature and cook for 5 minutes, then put on simmer until corn is done, 10 to 15 minutes. Add black pepper, to taste. If corn seems too dry, add a little milk or water.

FRUIT DIP

1 package (8 ounces) softened cream cheese
1 container (7 ounces) marshmallow creme

Use a mixer and beat together until smooth. Serve chilled with fresh fruit for dipping.

GARLIC & HERB
MASHED POTATOES

These go perfectly with Herb Roasted Prime Rib. They're creamy, herby, tummy warming goodness.

4 Potatoes
1/4 cup Skim Milk
1/4 cup Rondelé® by Président® Light Garlic & Herbs Gourmet Spread
4 Scallions chopped
Salt and Pepper

Peel and quarter the potatoes and add to a large pot of water. Cover and boil for 15 minutes. Drain the potatoes, place in large bowl, and add milk and Rondelé cheese. Mix until smooth. Garnish with scallions, and season to taste with salt and pepper.

MASHED CAULIFLOWER

1 head cauliflower, trimmed and cut into small florets
(about 6 to 7 cups)
2 tablespoons butter or olive oil
Salt

Bring a large pot of salted water to a boil. Add cauliflower
and cook about 10 to 15 minutes until very tender. Reserve
about 1/4 cup of cooking liquid. Drain cauliflower well.
Transfer cauliflower to a food processor. Add butter and
water, about a tablespoon at a time, and puree until smooth
and desired consistency. Season with salt and serve warm.

I slid into the booth and thumbed through the
menu. Despite my rumbling stomach, I decided
to stick with coffee. Mae expected us for dinner
in a couple of hours, and she'd smell restaurant
food on me a mile away.

— *Twelve Spirits of Christmas*

MOMMA'S CORN BREAD

2 cups white or yellow cornmeal
1/4 cup all-purpose flour
2 1/2 teaspoons baking powder
1/2 teaspoon baking soda
3/4 teaspoon salt
1 1/4 cups buttermilk
1 large egg
3 tablespoons melted shortening, plus more for the skillet

Heat the oven to 425°. Position the rack in the center of the oven. Put about 1 tablespoon of shortening in a 9- to 10 inch cast iron skillet and put the skillet in the oven.

In a large bowl, combine the cornmeal, flour, baking powder, soda, and salt. Whisk to blend thoroughly.

In another bowl, whisk together the buttermilk, egg, and shortening.

Add the buttermilk mixture to the dry mixture and stir just until blended. Carefully remove the hot cast iron pan from the oven and set it on a metal rack. Pour the batter into the sizzling shortening in the hot skillet.

Return the skillet to the oven, reduce the oven temperature to 375°, and bake for about 20 to 24 minutes, until golden brown.

Cut the cornbread into wedges and serve hot with soups, stew, chili, beans, or greens. Many people like to crumble their cornbread in a glass and fill it with cold milk. A pan of cornbread also makes a great dressing to go with chicken, pork, or turkey.

NUTS & BOLTS

6 tablespoons butter

4 tablespoons Worcestershire Sauce

1/2 shy teaspoon garlic powder (somewhere between 1/4 and 1/2 a teaspoon)

1/2 shy teaspoon salt

6 cups Wheat, Corn, or Rice Chex cereal (or any combination of the three)

3/4 cups salted nuts

1 cup Cheerios

1 cup pretzels

Preheat oven to 250. Melt butter in large pot. Add Worcestershire sauce, garlic, and salt. Add cereals, nuts & pretzels. Mix until evenly coated. Bake for 45 minutes, stirring every 15 minutes. Spread mixture onto paper towel or parchment paper to cool. Store in an airtight container.

OYSTER DRESSING

This is fabulous with the Brined Cajun Turkey!

Cornbread
- 1 cup self-rising cornmeal
- 1/2 cup self-rising flour
- 3/4 cup buttermilk
- 2 eggs
- 2 tablespoons vegetable oil

Dressing:
- 7 slices white bread, dried in warm oven
- Cornbread
- 1 sleeve saltine crackers
- 2 cups chopped celery
- 1 large onion, chopped
- 8 tablespoons butter
- 2 cups chicken stock
- 1 teaspoon salt
- 1/2 teaspoon freshly ground black pepper
- 1 teaspoon dried sage
- 1 tablespoon poultry seasoning
- 5 eggs, beaten
- 2 pints or 1 quart oysters, drained

Preheat oven to 350°.

To make the cornbread, combine all ingredients and pour into a greased shallow baking dish. Bake for approximately 20 to 25 minutes. Remove from oven and let cool. You can also buy Jiffy Cornbread Mix.

To make the dressing, crumble dried white bread slices, cornbread and crackers. Mix together and set aside.

Sauté chopped celery and onion in butter until transparent, approximately 5 to 10 minutes. Pour over corn bread mixture. Add stock, mix well and add salt, pepper, sage, and poultry seasoning. Add beaten eggs and mix well. Add oysters and mix. Pour into a greased pan. Bake for about 45 minutes.

PRALINE SWEET POTATO CASSEROLE

3 large sweet potatoes, peeled
3 eggs, beaten
1/2 cup of sugar
1 tablespoon vanilla
1/2 cup heavy cream or milk

Topping:
1 1/4 cups of chopped pecans
1 cup brown sugar
1/3 cup of flour
1 stick butter, melted

Preheat oven to 350°. Put sweet potatoes in a medium saucepan with water to cover. Boil until tender. Drain and mash. Let cool at bit. Mix the eggs, sugar, vanilla, and cream or milk with sweet potatoes. Mix well. Transfer to 2 quart casserole dish that has been sprayed with cooking spray. Mix together topping ingredients and on top of potato mixture. Bake for 30 to 40 minutes.

SAGE, SAUSAGE & APPLE DRESSING

16 ounce bag stuffing cubes
6 tablespoons unsalted butter, plus more for greasing the pan and topping
1 pound fresh sage sausage, casing removed
1 medium onion, chopped
2 cooking apples, peeled, cored, and chopped
1 to 2 ribs celery with leaves, chopped
1/2 teaspoon kosher salt
3 cups chicken broth, homemade or low-sodium canned
1/4 cup chopped fresh flat-leaf parsley
1/2 cup walnut pieces, toasted (See Note)
2 eggs, beaten

Preheat oven to 325°. Put the stuffing cubes in a large bowl and set aside. Butter a 3-quart casserole dish.

Melt 2 tablespoons of butter in a large skillet over medium-high heat. Add the sausage and break up with a wooden spoon. Cook until it loses most of its pink color, but not so much that it's dry, about 5 minutes. Add the sausage and pan drippings to the stuffing cubes. Melt the remaining butter in the pan. Add the onion, apple, celery, and salt. Cook until the vegetables get soft, about 5 minutes. Add the broth and parsley and bring to a boil.

Pour the vegetable mixture over the stuffing cubes and toss until evenly moistened. Mix in the walnuts and eggs. Loosely pack the dressing in the prepared pan and cook uncovered until the top forms a crust, about 40 minutes. Drizzle about 2 tablespoons of turkey pan drippings or melted butter over the top. Cook until the top is crisp and golden, about 20 minutes more. Set immediately or warm.

SAUSAGE BALLS IN CHEESE PASTRY

1 pound hot or mild pork sausage
3/4 cup dry breadcrumbs
1/3 cup chicken broth
1/8 teaspoon nutmeg
1/4 teaspoon poultry seasoning

Combine all ingredients in large bowl. Form into 1 teaspoon balls. Fry slowly on a low heat in a dry skillet until done. Frying too hot and fast will make the ball have a hard crust. Drain on paper towels.

Cheese pastry
1 1/2 cups all-purpose flour
1/4 teaspoon salt
1 teaspoon paprika
1/2 pound sharp cheddar cheese, shredded
1/2 cup softened butter

Mix flour, salt, and paprika in large bowl. Stir in cheese. Cut in butter. Work with hands until the dough is smooth. Pinch off about 1 tablespoon of dough and form around sausage ball. The balls may be baked immediately in a 375° oven for 15-20 minutes, or frozen unbaked until ready to use. If frozen, bake unthawed 400° 20-25 minutes. Makes about 45 balls.

SOUTHERN-STYLE GREEN BEANS WITH BACON AND NEW POTATOES

8 small new potatoes, halved if large
Salt and freshly ground black pepper
4 slices bacon, cut into thirds
1 medium onion, finely chopped
2 pounds fresh green beans, ends trimmed

In a large saucepan or medium Dutch oven, cook bacon over medium heat until it has rendered most of its fat and has begun to brown, about 5 minutes.

Add the onion and sauté until translucent, about 5 minutes. Add the green beans and potatoes and enough water to just cover them. Bring to a boil, then reduce the heat to low.

Season with salt and pepper, to taste, then cover the pan and simmer until the beans are very tender, about 1 hour, stirring occasionally and adding more water if necessary to keep the beans covered.

As the beans get close to being done they will become quite fragile, so take care when stirring.

SOUTHERN STYLE MAC 'N CHEESE

16 ounces macaroni, cooked al dente and drained
4 tablespoons butter, divided
5 cups shredded sharp cheddar cheese, divided
3 large eggs
1 teaspoon garlic salt
1/2 teaspoon black pepper
2 teaspoons Worcestershire sauce
3 cups half & half or milk
1/2 cup crushed butter crackers or Italian breadcrumbs
2 teaspoons dried parsley (optional)

Preheat oven to 350°. Toss hot macaroni with 2 tablespoons butter. Beat eggs, garlic salt, pepper and Worcestershire sauce together in a large bowl. Whisk in half and half. Place a half the macaroni in a 9 X 13 baking dish that has been sprayed with cooking spray.

Sprinkle 1 1/2 cups of the shredded cheese on top. Repeat with another layer of macaroni and 1 1/2 cups of cheese.

Pour egg mixture over macaroni and cheese. Stir a bit to coat pasta. Top with remaining 2 cups of cheese, crushed crackers or breadcrumbs and parsley.

Melt remaining 2 tablespoons butter and drizzle over the top. Bake covered with foil for 30 to 35 minutes. Uncover and bake another 10 to 15 minutes or until golden on top.

STUFFED MUSHROOMS

12 button mushrooms
3 tablespoons melted butter
1 small onion, chopped
1 cup breadcrumbs
1/2 cup chopped cooked chicken, ham, shrimp, bacon, pepperoni, or sausage
2 tablespoons cream or sherry
Salt and pepper to taste

Note - Seasonings such as Old Bay for shrimp or oregano for pepperoni can be added to taste. Get creative. You really can't mess these up!

Preheat broiler. Wash mushrooms and remove stems. Chop the stems and set aside.

In a skillet, heat 1 tablespoon butter, add the onion & chopped mushroom stems. Cook about 2 minutes. Add breadcrumbs, meat, seasonings, and enough liquid to moisten the mixture. DO NOT add too much! Remember when I said you couldn't mess these up? I lied. You can mess them up by making them too mushy.

Place mushrooms cup side down on a baking sheet and brush with 1 tablespoon butter. Broil 2 minutes. Flip the mushroom caps over and fill with stuffing. Brush with remaining butter and broil another 3 minutes.

SWEET POTATO BALLS

4 large sweet potatoes
2/3 cup packed brown sugar
2 tablespoons orange juice
1 teaspoon orange zest
1/2 teaspoon freshly grated nutmeg
2 cups shredded coconut, sweetened
1/2 cup granulated sugar
1 teaspoon ground cinnamon
1 large marshmallow per potato ball

Preheat oven to 350°. Bake the potatoes until tender, then peel and mash them.

Stir in the brown sugar, orange juice, zest and nutmeg. In a separate bowl, toss the coconut with the sugar and cinnamon.

Press mashed potatoes around each marshmallow, creating a 2 to 3 inch diameter ball. Roll the balls in the coconut mixture.

Bake for 15 to 20 minutes. Watch carefully for the last few minutes of cooking; the expanding marshmallows can cause the potato balls to burst open.

DESSERTS

I grabbed the bag, unfolded the first diaper, brought it to my face and sniffed. "Stop goofing around and help me. What kind of candy bar made this?"

Bryson's brows climbed into his hairline. "Excuse me?"

Realizing they had no idea how to play the game, I licked the poop smear inside the diaper.
Aaron turned his head and gagged.

"It's a candy bar! Come on help me. I'm not eating lettuce and chicken so I can get leftover brownie crumbs for dessert!"

— *The Spirit Child*

APPLE BUTTER PUMPKIN PIE

1 cup apple butter
1 cup fresh or canned pumpkin
1/2 cup packed brown sugar
1/2 teaspoon salt
3/4 teaspoon ground cinnamon
3/4 teaspoon ground nutmeg
1/8 teaspoon ground ginger
3 eggs, slightly beaten
3/4 cup evaporated milk
1 unbaked 9 inch pie shell
Sweetened whipped cream, for garnish

Preheat oven to 425°. Combine apple butter, pumpkin, sugar, salt and spices in a bowl. Stir in eggs. Gradually add milk and mix well. Pour into pie shell. Bake for about 40 minutes or until set.

Gram Mae's Secret: *If the crust begins to burn, place tin foil around the crust and lower the temperature of the oven. A tasty topping for this pie is praline pecans.*

APPLE CRISP WITH OATMEAL TOPPING

6 apples, peeled, cored, and sliced
2 tablespoons white sugar
1/2 teaspoon ground cinnamon
1/4 teaspoon nutmeg
1 cup brown sugar
3/4 cup old-fashioned oats
3/4 cup all-purpose flour
1 teaspoon ground cinnamon
1/2 cup cold butter
Caramels (optional but yummy)

Preheat oven to 350°. Toss apples with white sugar and 1/2 teaspoon cinnamon in a medium bowl to coat; pour into a 9 inch square baking dish. Add caramels.

Mix brown sugar, oats, flour, and 1 teaspoon cinnamon in a separate bowl. Use a pastry cutter or 2 forks to mash cold butter into the oats mixture until the mixture resembles coarse crumbs; spread over the apples to the edges of the baking dish. Pat the topping gently until even.

Bake in preheated oven until golden brown and sides are bubbling, about 40 minutes.

APPLE POUND CAKE

2 cups sugar
3 eggs
1 1/2 cups vegetable oil

Mix and beat together, then add the following.

3 cups flour
1 teaspoon salt
1 teaspoon baking soda
1 tablespoon butter or rum flavor extract

Mix the following in a separate bowl and add to the above mixture.

3 cups diced apples
1 cup chopped walnuts
1 cup coconut

Pour mixture into floured tube or bundt pan. Bake 1 hour and twenty minutes at 350°
For the Icing:
1/2 cup butter
1/2 cup cream
1 cup light brown sugar
1 teaspoon vanilla

Heat butter and sugar over low heat and bring to full boil. Cool 1 minute and add cream and vanilla. Pour over warm cake.

APPLE CARROT CAKE

4 eggs
2 cups sugar
1 1/2 cups vegetable oil

Mix the above ingredients together well.

2 cups plain flour
1 teaspoon salt
2 teaspoons soda

Sift the dry ingredients together in separate bowl. Then add to the egg mixture. Once smooth, add the following and stir well.

2 teaspoons cinnamon
1 teaspoon vanilla
1 cup grated fresh apples
1/2 teaspoon nutmeg
1/2 cup nuts chopped
1 cup grated carrot

Preheat oven 340°. Bake in greased 9x13 pan 25-30 minutes.

Icing:
1 box powdered sugar
1 teaspoon vanilla
1 8 ounce package of cream cheese
1/2 stick of butter

Beat until creamy and smooth over cooled cake.

"Go through the pecans and make sure there aren't any shells, then chop them into small pieces."

His eyes grew misty, and he turned his head. "That was my job every Christmas before my parents died."

"That's the wonderful thing about Christmas, every year you do the same things while reminiscing about doing them in years past. One Christmas, many years from now, you'll be shelling pecans and remember this conversation."

Aaron dipped his chin and grinned. "I thought you hated Christmas?"

"Maybe I needed someone to remind me of the good parts."

— Twelve Spirits of Christmas

BAILEY'S IRISH CREAM & COFFEE CHEESECAKE

1 1/2 cup graham cracker crumbs
6 tablespoon melted butter
1/4 cup granulated sugar
4 8 ounce packages cream cheese
1 cup granulated sugar
1 teaspoon vanilla
4 eggs
1 tablespoon instant coffee dissolved in 1 tablespoon hot water
1/4 – 1/2 cup Bailey's Irish Cream

Preheat oven to 350°. Stir together 1 1/2 cups graham cracker crumbs, 6 tablespoon melted butter, and 1/4 cup. granulated sugar.

Press crumbs onto bottom of springform pan (I used 10", but if you use a smaller one, your crust and cheesecake will just be higher) Bake for 8-10 minutes until toasted golden brown. Remove, and let cool while preparing filling. Beat 4 8 ounce. packages cream cheese that have been softened to room temperature with 1 cup granulated sugar until smooth and creamy. Add 1 teaspoon vanilla and beat in 4 eggs, one at a time.

Pour half the cheesecake filling into a separate bowl. To half of the batter, add 1 tablespoon instant coffee dissolved in 1 tablespoon hot water. To the other half of the batter, add 1/4 – 1/2 cup Bailey's Irish Cream, depending on how strongly Irish Creamy you want it.

Pour half of the Irish Cream filling into the crust. Very slowly, pour half of the coffee filling over the coffee filling. Repeat with the remaining halves of the Irish Cream and coffee fillings.

Gently run a spoon from the bottom of the filling to top without touching the crust to create a swirl.
Bake in preheated oven for 35-45 minutes, until center is barely set.

Remove from oven, run a knife around the edge to loosen it from the sides of the springform pan, and let cool completely in the pan.

BANANA BREAD (LOW FAT)

1 1/2 cups all-purpose flour
3/4 cup white sugar
1 1/4 teaspoons baking powder
1/2 teaspoon baking soda
1/2 teaspoon ground cinnamon
2 egg whites
1 cup banana, mashed
1/4 cup applesauce

Preheat oven to 350°. Lightly grease an 8x4 inch loaf pan. In a large bowl, stir together flour, sugar, baking powder, baking soda and cinnamon. Add egg whites, bananas and applesauce; stir just until combined. Pour batter into prepared pan.

Bake in preheated oven for 50 to 55 minutes, until a toothpick inserted into center of loaf comes out clean. Turn out onto wire rack and allow to cool before slicing.

BANANA BREAD OLD-FASHIONED

2/3 cup sugar
2/3 cup shortening
2 eggs
3 tablespoons buttermilk
1 cup mashed bananas
1 cup flour
1/4 teaspoon baking soda
1/2 cup nuts

Mix sugar, shortening, and eggs in blender. Add remaining ingredients and mix well. Pour into greased loaf pan. Bake 350° 45 minutes.

BANANA PUDDING

2 cups milk
2 eggs
2 heaping tablespoons flour
1 cup sugar
1/2 teaspoon salt
Bananas
1 box vanilla wafers
Whipped cream (about 2 cups)

Beat first five ingredients. Cook on low stirring constantly until thick. Cool. Make whipped cream and fold in 1 cup into pudding. Place in dish in the following manner: layer of wafers, pudding, bananas, wafers, repeat. Top with remaining whipped cream.

BOURBON BALLS

6 ounce bag chocolate chips
1/4 cup bourbon
2 1/2 cups finely crushed vanilla wafers
2 tablespoons corn syrup
1/4 cup water
1 cup chopped pecans
Powdered sugar

Melt chocolate in microwave or over a double boiler. Stir in syrup and bourbon. Add nuts and wafers. Mix well and let stand for 20 minutes. Make into small balls (about 50) and roll them in powdered sugar. Store in airtight container.

BROWNIE PIE

1 ready-made refrigerated pie crust
1/2 cup butter
2 ounces unsweetened chocolate, coarsely chopped
1 cup sugar
3/4 cup all-purpose flour
2 eggs
1 teaspoon vanilla extract
dash of salt
1 cup semi-sweet chocolate chips

Place Pie crust in a pie pan and set aside.

In a medium saucepan, melt butter over low heat. Add chocolate, stirring until completely melted.

Remove from heat and stir in sugar. Add flour, eggs, vanilla and salt. making sure all ingredients are mixed in well. Stir in chocolate chips.

Spread mixture into pie crust. Bake in a preheated 350° oven for 25 minutes, until top has a crust and sides are firm. Remove from oven and let cool completely.

BREAD PUDDING &
BOURBON SAUCE

4 large eggs
1 1/2 cups white granulated sugar
4 cups half and half
1 tablespoon vanilla extract
1 teaspoon ground cinnamon
1 (1 pound) loaf day-old French bread, torn into 1 inch chunks

Bourbon Sauce
   2 cups brown sugar
   1/2 cup butter
   1 1/2 cups heavy cream
   1 1/2 cups chopped pecans (optional)
   2 to 3 tablespoons Bourbon
   Pinch salt

In a mixing bowl, whisk together the eggs and sugar until light and creamy. Add the half and half, vanilla, and cinnamon. Whisk thoroughly until combined.

Spray 9 x 13 baking dish with cooking spray. Place bread in dish. Cover with the custard mixture. Use your clean hands to mix custard and bread together.

Let still out for 30 minutes to allow the bread to soak up the custard. You can also make a few hours ahead and cover and refrigerate until you're ready to bake.
Bake at 350° an hour or until set.

For Bourbon Sauce Melt butter in small saucepan over medium heat. Whisk in remaining ingredients. Simmer until thickened, whisking often, about 3 minutes. Cool slightly.

CAKE MIX CHOCOLATE COOKIES

1 box devil's food cake mix
1/3 cup vegetable oil
1 teaspoon vanilla
2 eggs
1/4 cup sugar

Heat oven to 350° (325° for dark or nonstick pans). In large bowl, mix cake mix, oil, vanilla and eggs with spoon until dough forms.

Refrigerate dough 15 to 30 minutes or as needed for easier handling. Shape dough into 1 inch balls; roll in sugar. On ungreased cookie sheets, place balls about 2 inches apart. Bake 9 to 11 minutes or until set. Cool 1 minute; remove from cookie sheets to cooling racks. Cool completely, about 30 minutes. Store tightly covered.

Mae slapped the table. "We have better things to do with our mouths than sex talk. Dig in, the food's getting cold."
— *Twelve Spirits of Christmas*

CARAMEL APPLE DUMP CAKE

1 box (15 ounces) yellow cake mix
2 cans (20 ounces each) apple pie filling
1 stick butter, melted
1/2 cup caramel sundae syrup (plus extra for drizzling on top)
Vanilla ice cream (optional)

Spray inside of crock pot with non-stick cooking spray or grease with butter or line with a slow cooker liner.

Dump cans of apple pie filling into bottom of crock pot, and spread evenly.

Evenly drizzle 1/2 cup caramel syrup over apple pie filling. In a medium mixing bowl, combine dry cake mix and melted butter, and stir until crumbly (break up large chunks into small crumbles using a spoon).

Pour butter/cake crumble mixture over the caramel apple pie filling layer in the crock pot, spread out evenly, and cover crock pot with lid.

Cook on HIGH for 2 hours, or LOW for 4 hours.

Serve up with vanilla ice cream and a drizzle of caramel on top.

Note - You can also bake this dessert in the oven. Preheat oven to 350°. Layer ingredients as instructed in a 9 x 13 inch pan. Bake 45 to 55 minutes or until golden.

CARIBBEAN BREAD PUDDING

1/4 cup butter
3 quarts Cuban bread cubes
2 1/2 cups eggs
1 1/4 cups sugar
5 cups milk
1 Tablespoons. vanilla extract
1/2 cup coconut rum
1/2 cup shredded coconut
1/2 cup canned pineapple, diced

Preheat oven 350°. Toss 3 tablespoons of melted butter with the bread cubes, place on a sheet pan and place in an oven at 350° and toast until golden. Brush a medium-sized casserole dish with one tablespoon of melted butter and add the toasted bread cubes. Mix all the remaining ingredients together and pour over the bread cubes. Press down on the bread cubes until they absorb most of the liquid. Bake hour or until firm in the center. Serve with ice cream and coconut rum sauce.

Coconut Rum Sauce
    1 1/2 cups heavy whipping cream
    2 egg yolks
    1/2 cup powdered sugar
    1/4 cup coconut rum

Add cream, egg yolks, and sugar to a small sauce pan on medium heat.
Stir constantly until the sauce starts to thicken, about 8 - 10 minutes.
Add the rum and stir. Pour into a container with a lid and place in an ice water bath. Chill ice bath in the refrigerator one hour.

CHOCOLATE CHIP COOKIES

1 cup butter, softened
3/4 cup packed light brown sugar
2 eggs
1 teaspoon baking soda
1 cup (12 ounce.) Hershey's semi-sweet chocolate chips
1 cup milk chocolate chips
1 cup butterscotch chips
3/4 cup granulated sugar
1 teaspoon vanilla
2 1/4 cup flour
1/2 teaspoon salt
1 cup chopped nuts (optional)

Cream butter, granulated sugar, brown sugar and vanilla in large mixer bowl until light and fluffy. Add eggs; beat well.

Combine flour, baking soda and salt; gradually add to creamed mixture. Beat well. Stir in chocolate chips and nuts.

Drop by teaspoonfuls onto greased cookie sheet.

Bake at 375° 8-10 minutes or until lightly browned. Cool slightly. Remove from cookie sheet; cool completely on wire rack.

Milk chocolate chips may be substituted for the semi-sweet chips.

CHOCOLATE MAYONNAISE CAKE

Frosting
- 1 pound semisweet chocolate chips
- 3 cups heavy cream
- Pinch fine salt

Cake
- Unsalted butter, for buttering the pan
- 2 cups all-purpose flour, plus more for the pan
- 2/3 unsweetened cocoa powder (not Dutch process)
- 1 1/4 teaspoons baking soda
- 1/4 teaspoon baking powder
- 1 tablespoon instant espresso powder
- 1 3/4 cups sugar
- 1 teaspoon pure vanilla extract
- 3 large eggs
- 1 cup mayonnaise
- 4 ounces semi-sweet chocolate chips, melted

For the Frosting
Put the chocolate in a large, heatproof bowl. Bring the cream to a boil in a medium saucepan over medium heat. Pour the hot cream over the chocolate and let it sit, undisturbed, for 10 minutes, then add the salt and stir until melted and combined.

Refrigerate, in the bowl, until thick and very cold, about 2 hours.

Whip with an electric mixer on medium-high until fluffy, spreadable and slightly lightened in color.

For the Cake

Preheat the oven to 350°. Butter and flour two 9 inch cake pans or line the bottom of each with parchment.

Combine the flour, cocoa powder, baking soda and baking powder in a medium bowl. Dissolve the instant espresso powder in 1 1/3 cups warm water.

Beat together the sugar, vanilla and eggs in a large bowl with an electric mixer on medium-high speed until light and fluffy, about 3 minutes. Beat in the mayonnaise and the melted chocolate until just combined.

Alternate beating the flour mixture and the espresso mixture on medium-high speed into the chocolate-egg mixture until just combined; work in 4 batches, beginning and ending with the flour mixture. Take care not to over mix.

Pour the cake batter into the prepared pans and bake until the cakes are set and the tops spring back when touched and a toothpick inserted into the center of the cakes comes out clean, about 30 minutes. Cool the cakes in the pans set on a rack for 20 minute. Invert the cakes onto the rack, remove the parchment paper and cool completely.

Frost the cake

Put 1 cake round on a cake stand or large serving plate and evenly spread 3/4 cup frosting over it. Top with the other cake round. Frost the top and sides with the remaining frosting. The cake can be frosted up to a day in advance. Let sit at room temperature for 30 minutes before serving.

CHOCOLATE TURTLES CHEESECAKE

2 cups vanilla wafer crumbs
2 tablespoons unsalted butter, melted
1 (14 ounce) package individually wrapped caramels
1 (5 ounce) can evaporated milk
1 cup chopped pecans
2 (8 ounce) packages cream cheese, softened
1/2 cup white sugar
1 teaspoon vanilla extract
2 eggs
1/2 cup semisweet chocolate chips

Preheat oven to 350°. In a large bowl, mix together the cookie crumbs and melted butter. Press into the bottom of a 9 inch springform pan.

In a heavy saucepan over low heat, melt the caramels with the evaporated milk. Heat and stir frequently until smooth. Pour caramel sauce into crust, and top with pecans.

In a large bowl, combine cream cheese, sugar and vanilla; beat well until smooth. Add eggs one at a time, mixing well after each addition. Melt the chocolate, and blend into cream cheese mixture. Pour chocolate batter over pecans.

Bake in preheated oven for 40 to 50 minutes, or until filling is set. Loosen cake from the edges of pan, but do not remove rim until cooled to prevent the top from cracking. Chill in refrigerator for 4 hours, or overnight.

Bryson turned and grinned. "She's kidnapped my dog."

"Looks that way for now. She'll send her back next time Maddie steals food off the table."

— *Twelve Spirits of Christmas*

COCONUT CAKE

1 1/2 cups sugar
1/2 cup shortening
2 eggs
2/3 cup milk or cream
2 cups flour
1/2 teaspoon salt
1 tablespoon baking powder
1/2 cup milk
1/2 teaspoon vanilla
1 teaspoon butter flavoring

Cream sugar and shortening together. Add eggs and beat until creamy. Ass 2/3 cup milk. Mix dry ingredients and add alternatively with remaining 1/2 cup milk and flavoring. Grease and flour 3 pans and bake 20-25 minutes at 350°.

Coconut filling
2/3 cup sugar
1 teaspoon flour
2 egg yolks
2/3 cup canned milk

Mix well and cook over medium low heat until it thickens. Remove from heat and add 2/3 cup coconut and 2 tablespoon butter. Pour this between the layers as you assemble the cake. Do not pour on top.

Frosting
- 1 cup sugar
- 2 egg whites
- 1 teaspoon vanilla
- 1/2 teaspoon vanilla
- 1/2 teaspoon cream of tartar
- 3 tablespoons water
- 2 6 ounce packages coconut

Mix sugar, cream of tartar, and water and cook until it forms a soft ball. Beat egg whites until very stiff and add hot mixture slowly to the beaten egg whites. Add vanilla and beat until fluffy. Spread on top and sides of cake and sprinkle coconut over the frosting.

I went to the kitchen in search of food and caffeine. Hunger and I didn't do well together, and coffee was the best defense against wayward spirits interrupting my personal thoughts.
— *Twelve Spirits of Christmas*

COCONUT PEACH DUMP CAKE

2 large cans (29 ounces each) peaches in syrup
1 box of yellow cake mix
1 stick butter, melted
3/4 cup of brown sugar
1 cup chopped pecans
1 cup shredded coconut

Preheat oven to 350°.

Spray 9 x 13 inch pan with cooking spray. Pour canned peaches with juice into pan. Pour cake mix over peaches. Drizzle butter over the top.

Sprinkle 3/4 cup brown sugar on top and bake for 30 minutes.

Top with chopped pecans and shredded coconut and bake for another 15 to 20 minutes. Best served warm with vanilla ice cream.

COLA CAKE

2 sticks butter, melted
1/2 cup oil
1 can cola
1/2 cup mini mashmallows
2 cups sugar
2 cups flour
1 teaspoon baking soda
2 1/2 cups cocoa
2 eggs
1 teaspoon vanilla
1/2 cup buttermilk

Add oil to melted butter, then add cola and let come to a boil. Add marshmallows and stir until melted, then add sugar, flour, baking soda, cocoa, eggs, buttermilk, and vanilla. Bake in a 13 x 9 inch pan at 350° 45 minutes.

Icing
Melt one stick of butter. Add 6 tablespoons cola and bring to a boil. Add 1 box powdered sugar, 1 cup nuts, 2 1/2 tablespoons cocoa, and 1 teaspoon vanilla. Pour over cake while it's hot.

CRANBERRY ORANGE LOAF

2 cups all-purpose flour
1 1/2 teaspoons baking powder
1/2 teaspoon baking soda
1/2 teaspoon salt
1 tablespoon grated orange zest
1 1/2 cups fresh cranberries
1/2 cup pecans, coarsely chopped
1/4 cup margarine, softened
1 cup white sugar
1 egg
3/4 cup orange juice

Preheat the oven to 350°. Grease and flour a 9 x 5 inch loaf pan. Whisk together flour, baking powder, baking soda, and salt. Stir in orange zest, cranberries, and pecans. Set aside.

In a large bowl, cream together margarine, sugar, and egg until smooth. Stir in orange juice. Beat in flour mixture until just moistened. Pour into prepared pan.

Bake for 1 hour in the preheated oven, or until the bread springs back when lightly touched. Let stand 10 minutes, then turn out onto a wire rack to cool. Wrap in plastic when completely cool.

DUMP CAKE

1 can cherry pie filling
1 can crushed pineapple, drained
A cup melted butter
1 package yellow cake mix
2/3 cup nuts, chopped
1 cup coconut

Preheat oven 350°. Spread pie filling evenly in the bottom of a greased 13x9 pan. Arrange drained pineapple over the cherry filling. Sprinkle cake mix over the pineapple. Cover with melted butter and top with nuts and coconut. Bake 1 hour. Serve hot or cold.

Mae continued, "It was Tessa's idea."
I looked at her with wide eyes. She'd lied at the table
with the same mouth she'd said grace.
"Isn't that right, Tessa?" Mae grinned.
                    — Twelve Spirits of Christmas

EGGNOG POUND CAKE

1 (16 ounce.) package pound cake mix
1 1/4 cups eggnog
2 large eggs
1/2 teaspoon freshly grated nutmeg
1/2 teaspoon vanilla extract

Preheat oven to 350°.

Beat all ingredients together at low speed with an electric mixer until blended. Increase speed to medium, and beat 2 minutes.

Pour into a lightly greased 9- x 5 inch loaf pan.
Bake at 350° 1 hour to 1 hour and 5 minutes or until a long wooden pick inserted in center comes out clean.
Cool in pan on a wire rack 10 minutes.

Remove from pan to wire rack, and cool completely (about 1 hour).

FANTASTIC FUDGE

3 (12 ounces each) packages semi-sweet chocolate chips
1 (7 ounce) container marshmallow cream or 4 cups mini marshmallows
2 sticks butter, softened
2 tablespoons vanilla extract
2 cups pecans or walnuts, chopped (optional)
4 1/2 cups sugar
1 (12 ounce) can evaporated milk

Line a 9 x 13 inch baking dish with foil. Spray foil with cooking spray. This makes it easier to remove the fudge and cut it.

Place chocolate chips, marshmallow cream, butter, vanilla, and nuts if using in large bowl. Set aside for later.

Pour sugar and evaporated milk in a large pot. Bring mixture to a boil and boil briskly for 7 minutes stirring continuously. You must stir to keep it from burning!

Remove from heat and pour into the bowl containing the chocolate chips mixture. Mix until incorporated completely. Pour into prepared pan and refrigerate until set.

GERMAN CHOCOLATE CAKE

1 box (15 ounces) German chocolate cake mix
1 box (3.5 ounces) instant chocolate pudding
1/2 cup vegetable oil
4 large eggs
1 1/4 cup water
Coconut Pecan Frosting
3/4 cup butter
1 1/2 cups sugar
1 can (10 ounces) evaporated milk
4 egg yolks, beaten
1 tablespoon vanilla
1 (7 ounce. package) sweetened flaked coconut
1 1/2 cups chopped pecans

Preheat oven to 350°.

Mix the cake mix, dry pudding mix, oil, eggs and water in a large mixing bowl on low speed for one minute until combined. Beat at medium speed for two minutes more.
Pour into 2 greased and floured 9 inch round pans.
Bake for 25 to 35 minutes or until the cake springs back when lightly pressed.

Allow to cool and remove from pans before frosting.

GERMAN CHOCOLATE PIE

4 ounces German sweet chocolate, chopped
1/4 cup butter, cubed
1 can (12 ounces) evaporated milk
1 1/2 cups sugar
3 tablespoons cornstarch
1/8 teaspoon salt
2 large eggs, lightly beaten
1 teaspoon vanilla extract
1 unbaked deep-dish pastry shell (9 inches)
1/2 cup chopped pecans
1 1/3 cups sweetened shredded coconut

In a microwave, melt chocolate and butter; stir until smooth. Gradually add milk; set aside.

In a large bowl, combine the sugar, cornstarch and salt. Stir in eggs and vanilla. Gradually stir in chocolate mixture. Pour into pastry shell.

Combine pecans and coconut; sprinkle over filling. Bake at 375° 45-50 minutes or until puffed and browned.

Cool 4 hours. Chill until serving (filling will become firm as it cools).

GORILLA BREAD

1/2 cup granulated sugar
3 teaspoons cinnamon
1/2 cup (1 stick) butter
1 cup packed brown sugar
1 (8 ounce) package cream cheese
2 (12 ounce) cans refrigerated biscuits (10 count)
1 1/2 cups coarsely chopped walnuts

Preheat the oven to 350°. Spray a Bundt pan with nonstick cooking spray.

Mix the granulated sugar and cinnamon. In a saucepan, melt the butter and brown sugar over low heat, stirring well. Set aside.

Cut the cream cheese into 20 equal cubes.

Press the biscuits out with your fingers and sprinkle each with 1/2 teaspoon of cinnamon sugar.

Place a cube of cream cheese in the center of each biscuit, wrapping and sealing the dough around the cream cheese. Sprinkle 1/2 cup of the nuts into the bottom of the Bundt pan.

Place half of the prepared biscuits in the pan. Sprinkle with cinnamon sugar, pour half of the melted butter mixture over the biscuits, and sprinkle on 1/2 cup of nuts.

Layer the remaining biscuits on top, sprinkle with the remaining cinnamon sugar, pour the remaining butter mixture over the biscuits, and sprinkle with the remaining 1/2 cup of nuts.

Bake for 30 minutes. Remove from the oven and cool for 5 minutes. Place a plate on top and invert.

INTERNATIONAL COFFEE CAKE

By Jackie Kennedy- Yes, THAT Jackie Kennedy.

1/2 cup butter
2 eggs
1 cup sugar
2 cups plain flour
1 teaspoon baking powder
1 teaspoon baking soda
1/2 teaspoon salt
1 cup sour cream
Topping
  1/3 cup brown sugar
  1/3 cup white sugar
  1/3 cup pecans
  1/2 teaspoon cinnamon
  2 tablespoons butter

Cream butter; add sugar; cream together. Add eggs, one at a time, beating well. Sift together flour, baking powder, baking soda and salt; add to first mixture, alternating with sour cream. Begin and end with flour mixture.

Stir in vanilla. In small dish, mix sugars, cinnamon and 2 tablespoons butter. Pour 1/2 of batter in greased bundt pan. Top with 1/2 sugar mixture. Pour in rest of batter and top with rest of sugar mixture. Bake at 325 ° for 45 minutes.

LEMON MOUSSE CHEESECAKE

Note - The water bath tempers the heat, creating the soft, creamy consistency. If you skip the water bath, the cheesecake will have a firmer, more traditional cheesecake texture.

Crust
   5tablespoons melted butter
   40 vanilla wafers, crushed, or 8 graham crackers, crushed (about 1 1/2 cups)
   1/4cup sugar

Filling
   24ounces cream cheese
   1 1/3cups sugar, divided
   1/3cup all-purpose flour
   4 eggs, separated
   1tablespoon finely grated lemon rind
   3/4cup lemon juice (about 4 lemons)

Preheat oven to 325F. To prepare crust, combine all ingredients. Stir well and press into a 10 inch springform pan.

Combine cream cheese and 1 cup sugar; beat until fluffy, about 5 minutes. Add flour, egg yolks, lemon rind and juice; beat until smooth. Beat egg whites until soft peaks form. Add remaining 1/3 cup sugar; beat until stiff peaks form. Fold into lemon batter. Pour batter into crust.

Place pan in a large baking pan. Add water to baking pan to a depth of 1 inch. Bake about 55 minutes, until cake is set but still jiggly in the center. Cover and chill at least 4 hours.

MONKEY BREAD

3 (8 ounce) packages of buttermilk biscuit tubes
1 cup sugar
2 teaspoons cinnamon
1 cup butter (2 sticks)
1/2 cup packed brown sugar

Generously grease Bundt pan with butter. Preheat oven to 350°. Cut each biscuit into four equal sized pieces. Combine 1 cup sugar and 2 teaspoons cinnamon in a bowl or plastic bag. Drop roll the pieces of dough in the sugar cinnamon mixture and gently arrange them into the prepared Bundt pan.

In a small sauce pan, combine 1/2 cup of the remaining sugar cinnamon mixture with 1/2 cup brown sugar and 1 cup butter. Bring mixture to a boil and then immediately remove from heat. Carefully drizzle the mixture over the rolled dough balls in the Bundt pan. Bake in preheated oven for 30 minutes.

Allow pan to rest for about 5 minutes, then cover with a large plate and invert bread. To eat, pull desired amount off with your fingers.

Gram Mae's Secret – Add nuts, chopped apples, drained peaches, pie filling, or other fruit for an unexpected treat.

MONSTER COOKIES

1 cup sugar
1 cup firmly packed brown sugar
1 cup peanut butter
1/2 cup or 1 stick butter, room temperature
3 large eggs
4 1/2 cups quick-cooking rolled oats
2 teaspoons baking soda
1 1/2 cups semisweet chocolate chips
1 1/2 cups M & M's

Preheat oven to 350°. In a large bowl or stand mixer, combine sugar, brown sugar, peanut butter and butter; beat until light and fluffy. Add eggs, 1 at a time, beating well after each addition.

Add oats and baking soda; mix well. Mix in chocolate chips and M & M's.

Drop dough by heaping tablespoons or bigger, depending on how "Monster" you want them, 2 1/2 inches apart onto ungreased cookie sheet.

Bake for 11 to 14 minutes or until light golden brown. Cool a few minutes and remove from cookie sheets.

NO FAIL PIE CRUST - SWEETER

4 cups all-purpose flour
1 tablespoon sugar
2 teaspoons salt
1 3/4 cups shortening
1/2 cup water
1 tablespoon vinegar
1 large egg

In large bowl, stir together with fork, flour, sugar and salt. Cut in shortening with fork until crumbly. In small bowl, beat together water, vinegar, and egg. Ass to flour mixture and stir until all ingredients are moistened.

Divide dough in 5 portions. Shape in flat round patty ready for rolling and wrap each patty in plastic or wax paper and shill at least 1/2 hour.

When ready to use, lightly flour both sides of patty. Roll out on floured board or pastry cloth. Roll out to 1/8 inch. Bake at 450.

Pie crust too crumbly?

1. *Too much fat or too little water*

2. *Insufficient blending of flour & fat*

3. *Use of self-rising flour without special recipe.*

NO FOOLS PIE

3/4 stick butter
1 cup self-rising flour
3/4 cup sugar
3/4 cup milk
1 1 1/2 cup drained fruit (your choice)

Melt butter in 8 or 9 inch pie plate in oven while oven is preheating to 350°.

Combine flour, sugar and 3/4 cup milk, stir until smooth. Pour batter over melted butter. Do not mix!

Place fruit over top of batter. Do not mix! Bake 30-40 minutes until lightly browned and center springs back when touched.

OATMEAL CHERRY COOKIES

2 sticks butter, softened at room temperature
1 cup firmly packed brown sugar
1/2 cup granulated sugar
2 large eggs
1 teaspoon vanilla extract
1 1/2 cups all-purpose flour
1/2 teaspoon salt
1 teaspoon baking soda
2 teaspoons cinnamon
3 cups old-fashioned oatmeal, uncooked
1 cup dried cherries

Preheat oven to 350°. Cream butter with sugars and beat until well blended.

Add eggs and vanilla, beat for several minutes until light and fluffy. Mix together flour, salt, baking soda, and cinnamon. Add them to the butter mixture and beat until well blended. Stir in oatmeal and cherries.

Drop batter by tablespoons onto un-greased or parchment lined cookie sheets. Bake until edges just turn golden, about 10 to 12 minutes.

Let cookies cool in the pan for a minute or two, then remove them to racks to cool.

PEACH COBBLER

1 cup self-rising flour
1 cup white sugar
1 cup milk
2 (16 ounce) cans sliced peaches in heavy syrup
1/2 cup butter

Preheat oven 350°. Melt butter or margarine in 9 x 13 inch pan. Mix together the flour, sugar, and milk. Pour mixture into the pan. Spread peaches, including syrup, evenly around the pan. Bake 30 to 40 minutes, until the crust turns golden brown. Let cool for about 10 minutes before serving.

PEANUT BUTTER COOKIES (NO FLOUR)

1 cup peanut butter
1 cup sugar
1 egg

Preheat oven 350°. Beat all the ingredients together. Drop onto baking sheets. Press down a bit with a fork. Bake 10-15 minutes. Cool about 10 minutes before eating.

PEANUT BUTTER KISS COOKIES

1/2 cup softened butter
1/2 cup creamy peanut butter
1 cup sugar, divided
1/2 cup brown sugar
1 egg
1 tablespoon milk
1 teaspoon vanilla extract
1 3/4 cups flour
1 teaspoon baking soda
1/2 teaspoon salt
30 to 40 chocolate Kisses, unwrapped

Preheat oven to 375°. In a large bowl, use a mixer to cream butter and peanut butter until light and fluffy. Gradually add 1/2 cup granulated sugar and brown sugar. Beat until light and fluffy. Add egg, milk, and vanilla extract. Beat well.

Add flour, baking soda, and salt. Mix well. Roll cookie dough into 1 inch balls. Roll balls in the remaining 1/2 cup sugar. Place balls, 2 inches apart, onto ungreased cookie sheets.

Bake 8 to 10 minutes or until lightly browned. Remove from oven and immediately press a chocolate kiss into the center of each. Put back in the oven for another 30 seconds. Remove from cookie sheet and let cookies cool. Makes about 3 dozen cookies.

PECAN PIE

1 pie crust, partially pre-baked
1 cup sugar
1 cup light corn syrup
1 teaspoon vanilla extract
1 teaspoon salt
1/4 teaspoon ground cinnamon
4 eggs, beaten
1 stick butter
2 cups pecans

Partially pre-bake a pie crust in a 9 inch pie pan according to instructions. Preheat oven to 350°.

In a medium bowl, whisk together brown sugar, corn syrup, salt; add eggs until smooth.

Melt butter in a small saucepan. Slowly pour butter into the sugar mixture, and whisk to combine. Stir in pecans, then pour filling into the prepared pie crust.

Bake for about 50-60 minutes, or until the filling is set. If the edges of the crust begin to turn too brown, briefly remove the pie from the oven and cover the crust with aluminum foil, then return to the oven. Once the filling is set, remove the pie and let cool completely before slicing. Great with whipped cream on top!

PERFECT PIE CRUST

3 cups flour
1/2 teaspoon. salt
1 1/4 cups shortening
5 tablespoons water
1 egg
1 teaspoon vinegar

Sift flour and salt. Cut in shortening until mixture looks like coarse cornmeal. Beat egg, water and vinegar together. Stir liquid into flour mixture. Gather into a ball. Chill. Divide dough into 4 small balls. Roll out on floured board to fit pie pan. Bake in 425° oven for 10 to 12 minutes. Makes 4 single pie crust or two double crust. This is a never fail pastry recipe.

PINEAPPLE NUT BREAD

1/2 cup shortening
1 1/2 cups firmly packed brown sugar
2 eggs
4 cups flour
1 can crushed pineapple
1 can frozen orange juice concentrate (thawed)
2 teaspoons sugar
1/4 teaspoon salt
1/2 cup nuts (optional)

Cream sugar and shortening until light. Add eggs, beat well. Sift flour, soda, and salt. Add orange juice to dry ingredients and mix well. Stir in nuts and pineapple. Turn out into two greased and floured loaf pans. Bake 350°, 50-60 minutes.

PINEAPPLE UPSIDE DOWN CAKE

1 stick butter

1 1/4 cups packed brown sugar

1 can (20 ounces) pineapple slices in juice, drained (save the juice)

1 large can (or two small) crushed pineapple, drained (save the juice)

1 jar (6 ounces) maraschino cherries without stems, drained

1 box yellow cake mix, batter prepared according to box directions

Preheat oven to 350°.

Melt butter and sugar together in a saucepan over low heat. When the sugar has melted, add crushed pineapple. Stir to combine. Remove from heat and pour mixture into a greased 9" x 13" pan or 2 greased 8 inch round pans.

Arrange pineapple slices on top of brown sugar mixture. Place cherry in center of each pineapple slice and arrange remaining cherries around slices.

Make cake batter as directed on box, except substitute pineapple juice for water. If you don't have enough juice, add water to yield the amount needed for the cake mix. Spoon batter over pineapple and cherries.

Bake 45 to 50 minutes or until toothpick inserted in center comes out clean. Immediately run knife around side of pan to loosen cake. Place heatproof serving plate upside down onto pan and turn plate and pan over. Leave pan over cake 5 minutes and remove.

Gram Mae's Secret – There's nothing wrong with doubling the amount of brown sugar and butter to make this cake extra rich. Likewise, add a half cup of rum to the brown sugar mixture for a more grown up flavor.

Something about watching a guy stuff his face made me happy. Maybe it was because I was raised in a house where dinner was an event, and nothing ever came out of a box unless it was pizza.

"Save room for dessert," I told him.

"No worries there. I have a separate stomach for sweets." He winked and took another bite.
— *The Spirit Tree*

POPPY SEED BREAD

This is a Czechoslovakian dessert or breakfast dish that has a unique flavor and a hint of sweetness. Serve slices warm and smeared with butter.

 1/2 cup butter
 1/4 cup sugar
 1/2 teaspoon salt
 2 envelopes of dry yeast
 3/4 cup very warm water
 2 teaspoons grated lemon rind
 3 cups sifted all-purpose flour
 1 can poppy seed filling

Combine butter (save the wrapper), sugar and salt in small sauce-pan. Heat slowly, stirring often until the butter melts. Cool to lukewarm.

Dissolve yeast and 1 teaspoon sugar in very warm water in large bowl. Stir until well blended and allow to stand 10 minutes until the mixture begins to bubble. Stir in cooled butter mixture and lemon rind. Beat in enough flour to make a soft dough. Turn out onto lightly floured surface. Knead until smooth and elastic (about 5 minutes) use remaining flour to keep the dough from sticking to the counter and your hands. Place in a buttered bowl (use the wrapper from the butter to butter the bowl.) Cover with a clean towel. Let rise in a warm place about 1 hour.

Punch a hole in the dough, turn out on floured surface, knead and roll out. Fill with poppy seed filling. Let rise again for about an hour. Bake at 350° 40 minutes.

PUMPKIN BREAD

3 eggs, beaten
2 cups sugar
1 can (15 ounces) pumpkin
2 sticks butter, melted
1 tablespoon vanilla
3 cups flour
1 teaspoon baking soda
1/2 teaspoon baking powder
1/2 teaspoon salt
1 teaspoon cinnamon
2 teaspoons pumpkin pie spice
1 cup chopped walnuts (optional)

Preheat oven 350°. In a bowl, whisk together the first 5 ingredients. Whisk together dry ingredients in another bowl. Gradually add to dry ingredients to pumpkin mixture. Mix well. Stir in the nuts.

Spoon batter into 2 9 inch loaf pans that have been sprayed with cooking spray. Bake 45 to 55 minutes. Cool about 10 minutes before removing from the pans. Makes 2 loaves.

RED VELVET CAKE

1/2 cup shortening
1 1/2 cups sugar
2 eggs
2 ounces red food coloring
2 heaping tablespoons cocoa
1 cup buttermilk
2 1/4 cups cake flour
1 teaspoon salt
1 teaspoon vanilla
1 teaspoon baking soda
1 teaspoon vinegar

Preheat oven 350°. Cream shortening, sugar and eggs. Make a paste of food coloring and cocoa. Add to creamed mixture. Add buttermilk alternating with flour and salt. Add vanilla. Add soda to vinegar, and blend into the batter. Pour into 3 or 4 greased and floured 8" cake pans. Bake 24-30 minutes.
Split layers fill and frost with the following frosting.

Frosting
    3 tablespoons flour
    1 cup milk
    1 cup sugar
    1 teaspoon vanilla
    1 cup butter (DON'T use margarine or other butter substitutes)

Add milk to flour slowly, avoiding lumps. Cook flour and milk until very thick, stirring constantly. Cool completely. Cream sugar, butter and vanilla until fluffy. Add to cooked mixture. Beat, high speed, until very fluffy. Looks and tastes like whipped cream.

RUM BALLS

Watch out. Because you're not cooking out the alcohol, these pack a punch!

1 box vanilla wafers, finely crushed (12 ounces box = 3-1/2 cups)
4 tablespoons unsweetened cocoa powder
2 cups chopped nuts
1 box confectioners' (powdered) sugar
1 stick of butter, melted
1/2 cup rum
1/4 cup light corn syrup
Extra confectioners' (powdered) sugar for coating

Mix dry ingredients in a large bowl. Mix rum and syrup together, then add to dry ingredients. Add the melted butter and stir to moisten. Mold into balls and dredge in confectioners' sugar.

These are best stored in a tightly sealing metal box and left to 'ripen' for a few days.

SEVEN LAYER COOKIE BARS

1 1/2 cups graham cracker crumbs
1/2 cup butter or margarine, melted
1 (14 ounce) can sweetened condensed milk
1 cup semi-sweet chocolate chips
1 cup butterscotch-flavored chips
1 1/3 cups flaked coconut
1 cup chopped nuts

Preheat oven to 350° (325° for glass baking pan). In small bowl, combine graham cracker crumbs and butter; mix well. Press crumb mixture firmly on bottom of 13x9 inch baking pan.

Pour sweetened condensed milk evenly over crumb mixture. Layer evenly with remaining ingredients; press down firmly with fork.

Bake 25 minutes or until lightly browned. Cool. Chill if desired. Cut into bars or diamonds. Store covered at room temperature.

STRAWBERRY BREAD

1/2 cup butter, softened
1 cup sugar
4 ounces cream cheese, softened
2 eggs
1/2 cup milk
1 teaspoon vanilla extract
2 cups flour
2 teaspoons baking powder
1/2 teaspoon baking soda
1/2 teaspoon salt
2 cups strawberries, chopped

Preheat oven to 350°. With electric mixer cream butter, sugar and cream cheese until fluffy. Add eggs one at a time. Beat in milk and vanilla.

In separate bowl, mix flour, baking powder, baking soda and salt. Blend flour mixture with butter mixture just until blended.

Gently fold in the strawberries being careful not to over mix.

Grease and flour a 9×5 inch loaf pan. Bake for 50 to 60 minutes or until cooked through and golden on top. Let cool just a bit before removing from pan and slicing.

STRAWBERRY CAKE

This cake is my absolute favorite. My great-grandmother made this for me on my sixth birthday, and I never forgot it. It's pink and pretty and sweet – all it's missing is a unicorn horn.

1 (18.25 ounce) box white cake mix
1 (3 ounce) box strawberry-flavored instant gelatin
1 (15 ounce) package frozen strawberries in syrup, thawed and pureed
4 large eggs
1/2 cup vegetable oil
1/4 cup water

Preheat oven to 350°. Lightly grease 2 (9 inch) round cake pans.

In a large bowl, combine cake mix and gelatin. Add pureed strawberries, eggs, oil, and water; beat at medium speed with an electric mixer until smooth. Pour into prepared pans, and bake for 20 minutes, or until a wooden pick inserted in the center comes out clean.

Let cool in pans for 10 minutes. Remove from pans, and cool completely on wire racks.

Strawberry Cream Cheese Frosting
    1/4 cup butter, softened
    1 (8 ounce) package cream cheese, softened
    1 (10 ounce) package frozen strawberries in syrup, thawed and pureed
    1/2 teaspoon strawberry extract
    7 cups confectioners' sugar

Freshly sliced strawberries, for garnish, optional

In a large bowl, beat butter and cream cheese at medium speed with an electric mixer until creamy. Beat in 1/4 cup of the strawberry puree and the strawberry extract. (The rest of the puree is leftover but can be used in smoothies or on ice cream for a delicious treat.) Gradually add confectioners' sugar, beating until smooth.

Spread frosting in between layers and on top and sides of cake. Garnish with sliced fresh strawberries, if desired.

TEX-MEX S'MORES

Flour tortillas
Peanut butter
Chocolate chips
Miniature marshmallows

Spread peanut butter on tortillas. Add a handful of chocolate chips and marshmallows. Fold tortilla in half and wrap in foil. Cook on grill over low heat, or in a 300° oven for 3-5 minutes. Unwrap and enjoy.

TURTLE PUMPKIN PIE

1/3 cup caramel ice cream topping
1 ready-to-use graham cracker crust
1/2 cup chopped pecans
2 packages (3.4 ounce each) instant vanilla pudding mix
1 cup cold milk
1 cup canned pumpkin
1 teaspoon ground cinnamon
1/2 teaspoon ground nutmeg
1 (8 ounce) tub Cool Whip, thawed

Pour caramel topping onto bottom of pie crust; sprinkle with pecans.

In a large bowl, beat together pudding mixes, milk, canned pumpkin, cinnamon, and nutmeg.

Mix 1 1/2 cups Cool Whip to the pumpkin mixture. Spoon into crust. Refrigerate 1 hour. Top pie with remaining Cool Whip, then drizzle with additional caramel topping and pecans (optional) before serving.

WHITE CHOCOLATE, COCONUT & MACADAMIA NUT COOKIES

2 cups, plus 2 tablespoons flour
1/2 teaspoon baking soda
1/4 teaspoon salt
1 1/2 sticks butter, melted
1 cup brown sugar
1/2 cup sugar
1 whole egg
1 egg yolk
2 teaspoons vanilla
1 1/2 cups white chocolate chips
1 1/2 cups sweetened shredded coconut
1 cup chopped macadamia nuts

Preheat oven to 325°. Line a cookie sheet with parchment paper or spray well with cooking spray. Mix together flour, baking soda and salt in a small bowl. Use a mixer to beat butter and sugars together. Add egg, egg yolk, and vanilla. Beat again. Add dry ingredients. Beat on low. Mix in chips, coconut and nuts.

Use an ice cream or large cookie scoop to scoop out about 1/4 cup of dough and roll into a ball. Place on a cookie sheet and flatten a bit. Bake for 7 to 8 minutes on top rack of the oven. Then, move pan to the bottom rack and bake another 7 to 10 minutes.

WHITE CHOCOLATE RASPBERRY CHEESECAKE RECIPE

1 1/2 cups graham cracker crumbs
1/4 cup sugar
1/3 cup butter, melted

Filling
3 packages (8 ounces each) cream cheese, softened
3/4 cup sugar
1/3 cup sour cream
3 tablespoons all-purpose flour
1 teaspoon vanilla extract
3 large eggs, lightly beaten
1 package (10 to 12 ounces) white baking chips
1/4 cup seedless raspberry jam

In a small bowl, combine the graham cracker crumbs, sugar and butter. Press onto the bottom of a greased 9-in. springform pan; set aside.

In a large bowl, beat cream cheese and sugar until smooth. Beat in the sour cream, flour and vanilla. Add eggs; beat on low speed just until combined. Fold in the chips. Pour over crust.

In a microwave, melt raspberry jam; stir until smooth. Drop by teaspoonfuls over batter; cut through batter with a knife to swirl.

Place pan on a double thickness of heavy-duty foil (about 18 in. square). Securely wrap foil around pan. Place in a large baking pan; add 1 in. of hot water to larger pan.

Bake at 325° 80-85 minutes or until center is just set. Cool on a wire rack for 10 minutes. Carefully run a knife around edge of pan to loosen; cool 1 hour longer. Cover and refrigerate overnight. Remove sides of pan.

Aaron watched the redneck parade with wide eyes. "You're related to all of them?"

Could it be the prospect of facing the entire famn damily worried my unflappable police detective? "Most of them. Some aren't blood. Gram Mae has a way of picking up strays."

He slipped his arms around me and whispered, "Just like her great granddaughter."
— *The Spirit Child*

ALSO BY KATHRYN M. HEARST

Tessa Lamar Novels

The Spirit Tree

Twelve Spirits of Christmas

The Spirit Child

Sinistra Dei Series

Feast of Reverence

Feast of the Epiphany

Feast of Mercy

Feast of Atonement (Summer 2018)

Feast of Ascension (Fall 2018)

Zodiac Shifters

Dragon Glass

Contemporary Romance

Going Dark

Bourbon Street Bad Boys Club Series

(Coming soon)

Made in the USA
Columbia, SC
06 December 2021